Five Minute Biographies For Your Success

Dale Carnegie

Five Minute Biographies For Your Success

1판 4쇄 발행 2010년 7월 19일
개정판 1쇄 발행 2012년 5월 16일
개정판 2쇄 발행 2012년 9월 10일

지은이 | Dale Carnegie
주석 | 노태복
펴낸이 | 박찬영
기획편집 | 이인석, 김혜경, 성이경
마케팅 | 이진규, 장민영
관리 | 한미정
디자인 | 이창욱

발행처 | 리베르
주소 | 서울시 용산구 용산동5가 24번지 용산파크타워 103동 505호
등록번호 | 제2003-43호
전화 | 02-790-0587, 0588
팩스 | 02-790-0589
홈페이지 | www.리베르.com
e-mail | skyblue7410@hanmail.net

ISBN | 978-89-6582-035-2 (14740)

copyright©LIBER, 2008

리베르(Liber 로마의 신)는 자유와 지성을 상징합니다.

Five Minute Biographies

For

Your Success

Dale Carnegie

라베르

머리말

　데일 카네기는 『자기관리론』 『인간관계론』 등의 저서로 유명한 미국의 자기계발 전문가다. 많은 독자들이 그의 책을 성공적이고 행복한 삶을 향한 여정의 이정표로 삼고 있다. 카네기의 저서를 통해 수많은 독자들이 삶의 지혜를 얻고 있는 가운데 아직 국내에 소개되지 않은 『데일 카네기 1% 성공습관』 (Five Minute Biographies For Your Success)의 번역본이 원본 텍스트와 함께 출간된 것은 여간 반가운 소식이 아니다.

　『데일 카네기 1% 성공습관』은 현대사의 위인들과 명사들의 삶을 간략히 조명하면서 삶의 지혜와 행복의 길을 손에 잡힐 듯이 제시해준다. 번역본만으로도 독자들은 저명한 인물들의 삶의 여정에 동참하는 값진 경험을 할 수 있지만, 영어 텍스트를 통해 양자를 대조해서 읽으면 고급스러운 영어도 자연스레 습득하게 된다. 특히 카네기의 글들은 고등학교 교과서에도 수록됐을 정도로 표준적인 영어로 쓰여 있어 더욱 영어 학습에 도움이 될 것이다.

　삶의 지혜와 수준 높은 영어, 현대에 꼭 필요한 이 두 가지를 함께 체득하고 싶은 독자들께는 번역본과 더불어 이 영어 텍스트가 귀중한 선물이 될 것이다.

『데일 카네기 1% 성공습관』 옮긴이 노태복

Contents

1. The World's Most Famous Woman Scientist Once Slept Under a Chair to Keep Warm
   MADAME CURIE — 12

2. The Deaf, Dumb and Blind Girl Who Was Likened to Napoleon
   HELEN KELLER — 24

3. He Made More Millionaires Than Any Man Who Ever Lived
   ANDREW CARNEGIE — 31

4. She Turned Him Down Because He Had "No Prospects"—His Name Was John D.!
   JOHN D. ROCKEFELLER — 40

5. He Knew the Telephone Numbers of More Beautiful Girls Than Any Man in History
   FLORENZ ZIEGFELD — 47

6. His Peasant Mother Went Barefoot to Pay For His Music Lessons and He Became the Greatest Singer in the World
   ENRICO CARUSO — 57

7. "He Sought the Secrets of the Pole—He Found the Secrets of God"
   CAPTAIN ROBERT FALCON SCOTT — 66

8. He Once Picked Grapes to Pay His Rent—Today His Voice Is Worth a Fortune
   LAWRENCE TIBBETT — 73

9. Shakespeare Had a Shot-Gun Wedding
   WILLIAM SHAKESPEARE — 81

10. He Went to School For Only Four Years —Yet He Wrote Seventeen Immortal Novels
CHARLES DICKENS 88

11. He Refused to Invest Money in a Newfangled Contraption Called the Telephone
MARK TWAIN 96

12. Three Little Words —"Can You Cook?" —Led Him to the Ends of the Earth
MARTIN JOHNSON 111

13. The Missionary Who Got on the Wrong Train —and Became a Famous Magician
HOWARD THURSTON 121

14. Two-Cent Newspapers Bought Him Castles in Spain, Cuckoo Clocks, and Egyptian Mummies
WILLIAM RANDOLPH HEARST 129

15. At 26 He Was a Star; at 53 a Has-Been; at 57 the Greatest Actor in America
LIONEL BARRYMORE 136

16. The Play That "Wasn't Worth Bothering About" Became the Greatest Drama Since Hamlet
SOMERSET MAUGHAM 142

17. A Small-Town Insult Made Him the Greatest Criminal Lawyer of His Time
CLARENCE DARROW 149

18. Stick His Head in a Lion's Mouth? —Not without a Gas Mask!
CLYDE BEATTY 156

19. The Ill-Wind That Wrecked a Whole Town—and May Yet Save the World from Insanity
THE MAYO BROTHERS   165

20. He Was Ashamed of Having Written Two of the World's Greatest Novels
LEO TOLSTOY   173

21. They Came After Him With Guns and T.N.T.—But He Still Raised Easter Lilies
J. PIERPONT MORGAN   180

22. The Spinster Who Turned Down the Marriage Proposals of a Thousand Men and Rode a Snorting, Bucking Horse
EVANGELINE BOOTH   189

23. The Ballplayer Who Led a Million Souls Down the Sawdust Trail to Salvation
BILLY SUNDAY   197

24. He Was Shot in the Breast; But He Kept Right on With His Speech
THEODORE ROOSEVELT   204

25. He Was Faced With One of the Greatest Opportunities in History; Yet He Failed Because He Couldn't Handle People
WOODROW WILSON   211

26. The "Tough Guy" Who Went Through High School in Three Months and Wrote Fifty-One Books in Eighteen Years
JACK LONDON   218

27. He Got $49.49 a Word—For a Book He Was Sorry He Ever Wrote!
CHIC SALE   226

28. What The Movies Didn't Tell About the Bengal Lancer
FRANCIS YEATS-BROWN   233

29. Once Doomed to Die for Want of Ten Cents —He Lived to Tear Up $1,000,000
AL JOLSON   242

30. Fired from Four Newspapers—He Won the Nobel Prize and Thought It Was a Gag
SINCLAIR LEWIS   249

31. He Offered a Million Dollars For a Bride
DIAMOND JIM BRADY   257

32. She Resold Her Morning Paper and Spent Hours in the July Sun Sorting Rags, to Increase Her Fortune of $65,000,000
HETTY GREEN   265

33. He Earned Five Thousand Dollars a Day, Yet He Searched Garbage Cans for Food for His Pet Vulture
JOHN BARRYMORE   271

34. He Stepped Outside for a Fight —While He Was Gone He Broke the Bank and Won $10,000!
ELY CULBERTSON   283

35. New York's Queerest Rich Family
THE WENDEL FAMILY   290

36. The Mystery Man Who May Have Been Responsible for the Death of Someone You Know
BASIL ZAHAROFF   299

37. The "Perfect Lover" Who Chewed Tobacco, Bit His Fingernails, and Drank Wine Out of Human Skulls
LORD BYRON   306

★ Words & Phrases   315

This book is dedicated to a successful man
who is never in a hurry

WARREN S. BARLOW

MADAME CURIE

THE WORLD'S MOST FAMOUS WOMAN
SCIENTIST ONCE SLEPT UNDER A CHAIR TO KEEP WARM

⁓ MADAME CURIE, of the very few women whose names will probably be remembered for a thousand years, was a shy, timid Polish girl who discovered what the great scientists thought was impossible. She discovered a new element vastly different from any other element known to science—an element that radiated energy incessantly. She named it radium.

Radium's greatest contribution is in the war we are waging against cancer. Countless thousands of cancer patients have either been permanently cured by radium or have had their terrible suffering alleviated, and in many cases their lives lengthened by many years.

While the future Madame Curie was studying physics and mathematics in the University of Paris, she was so poor that she actually fainted from hunger. Wouldn't she have been astonished then if she could have known that fifty-two years later a motion picture company would spend over a million dollars making a picture of her life! Wouldn't she have been astonished if she could have foreseen that she was to become the only person who has twice been given the Nobel Prize for achievement in science! The first time was in 1903 for her outstanding achievement in physics, and the second time in 1911 for her outstanding achievement in chemistry.

Yet Madame Curie probably would never have

become a scientist at all nor ever have discovered radium if she had not been insulted, as a young girl, by an arrogant and wealthy family in her native Poland.

The story goes like this:

When the future Madame Curie was a young girl of nineteen, she was employed by a wealthy family in Poland to look after their ten-year-old daughter, to care for her and help her in her studies. When the eldest son of this rich family came home from college for the Christmas holidays, he danced and skated with the new governess; he was charmed by her beautiful manners and delighted with her sparkling wit and poetry. He fell in love with her and proposed marriage, but when his mother heard the news she almost fainted; his father stormed and raged.

What! His son proposing to marry a girl without a penny! A girl without social standing, a girl employed in other people's homes!

The future Madame Curie was stunned by this disgraceful slap in the face—so stunned that she resolved to abandon all thoughts of marriage and to go to Paris to study and devote her life to science.

In 1891 this young Polish woman—Manya Sklodowska she was then—registered for the science course at the University of Paris. She was too shy and timid to make friends, and she was so terribly in earnest she had no time for friends. Every moment she could not consecrate to her studies, she considered lost. For the next four years she had to live on the little money she had saved as a governess, plus the few rubles that her father, a teacher of mathematics in Poland, could send her now and then. She had to live on sixty cents a day—pay for her room, her food, clothes, heat, and expenses at the university. Her room had only one window and that was a skylight. It had no gas, no electric light, and, what was a thousand times worse, it had no heat. She could afford to buy only two sacks of coal throughout the entire winter.

To save her little treasure of coal, she often did not light the stove on winter nights, working her mathematical problems with fingers that were numb and shoulders that were shaking. Then before she went to bed, the future Madame Curie would open her trunk and take out her towels, pillow cases, a sheet, her extra dress, and pile all these things on top of her bed in order to keep warm. But still she shivered. Occasionally she reached for her chair and pulled it on top of the bed, hoping desperately that somehow even a chair would add a bit of warmth to her shaking body.

Not only did she have little food to cook, but she felt it was stealing precious time away from her studies to cook even the little that she had. For weeks at a time she forced her body to get along on nothing but a little bread and butter and weak tea. Often she grew dizzy, stumbled to her bed, and lost consciousness. When she came to her senses, she would ask herself: "Why did I faint?" She was unwilling to admit that her disease was slow starvation. Once she fainted in a class at the University, and when she regained consciousness, she admitted to the doctor that she had lived for days on a few cherries and a bunch of radishes.

But let's not feel too sorry for this student in her Paris garret—this student who was destined ten years later to become the most famous woman in the world. She was so absorbed in her work, so obsessed by a desire for knowledge, that hunger could not make her falter, nor cold dampen the fires that burned within.

Three years after she arrived in Paris, Manya Sklodowska married the only kind of man with whom she could ever have been happy—a man who, like herself, was completely devoted to science. His name was Pierre Curie. He was only thirty-five years old, yet he was one of the most distinguished scientists in France.

The day they were married their total earthly possessions consisted of a couple of bicycles, and they spent their honeymoon bicycling through the French country-side, lunching on bread and cheese and fruit, and spending their nights in village inns where the soft candlelight threw weird shadows on the faded wallpaper.

Three years later, Madame Curie was preparing for her doctor's degree; in order to get the degree of Doctor of Philosophy, she had to do some original scientific research and write a report on it. She decided to devote her research to trying to solve a recently discovered mystery—the mystery of why a metal called uranium gave off rays of light.

It was the beginning of a great scientific

adventure, a voyage into the fascinating mysteries of chemistry.

Madame Curie tested all known chemical bodies and she also tested hundreds of minerals to discover if they gave off those mysterious rays; she finally concluded that these powerful rays were shot into space by some unknown element.

Finally, Madame Curie's husband, Pierre Curie, dropped his own experiments to help her search for this mysterious new element.

After months of experiment, Madame Curie and her husband tossed a bombshell into the scientific world. They announced that they believed they had discovered a metal whose radiation was two million times stronger than the radiation of uranium; a metal whose rays could penetrate wood, stone, steel, copper; a miracle metal whose rays could be stopped by nothing except thick sheets of lead. If they had indeed made such a discovery, it would upset all the fundamental theories in which scientists had believed for centuries.

They named their miraculous substance radium.

Nothing remotely like it had ever been known before. It was so sensationally different from all other metals that sober scientists doubted that such a metal could even exist. They demanded proof. Show us pure radium, they said, so we can see it and test it and discover its atomic weight.

So Madame Curie and her husband worked for the next four years(1898 to 1902) to prove the existence of radium—worked for four years to produce a decigram of radium, a quantity no bigger than half the size of a small pea.

How did they produce it? By boiling down and refining eight tons of ore. They worked in an old abandoned shed that had formerly been used by medical students as a dissecting room; it had been deemed no longer fit for even that work. It had no floor, a leaky roof, an old and totally inadequate stove; in the winter time it was as cold as all outdoors. The bitter smoke from the boiling ores and chemicals stung Madame Curie's eyes and choked her throat. For four years she and her husband worked in that miserable shed. He finally grew discouraged and wanted to give up the search until some more favorable time, but Madame Curie refused to quit; so they persisted until they had actually produced a decigram of radium.

As a result of that discovery, Madame Curie became the most famous and the most distinguished woman on earth. But were those days of glory and honor her happiest? Ah, no; she declared that the happiest years of her life had been the poverty-stricken years when she was working in that miserable old shed with a dirt floor—years when her body often shivered with cold and collapsed with fatigue, but years entirely consecrated to work she loved.

In 1902 Madame Curie and her husband had to decide whether they wanted to be rich, or true to the selfless ideals of scientific research. By that time it had already been discovered that radium was invaluable in treating cancer. There was a growing demand for radium and no one else in the world knew how to produce it except Madame Curie and her husband. They could have patented the technique they had invented for extracting it and have obtained a royalty on every bit of radium produced throughout the world.

Since radium was going to be produced for a profit, few people would have blamed Madame Curie and her husband for accepting a royalty from the commercial manufacturers. Such a royalty would have meant economic security for them and their children, the elimination of drudgery, and the building of a fine laboratory for further research.

But it renews and deepens one's faith in human nature to know that Madame Curie refused to accept one penny for her discovery. "It would be impossible," she said. "It would be contrary to the scientific spirit. Besides, radium is going to be used in treating disease, and it would be impossible to take advantage of that."

So, with Christlike unselfishness, she chose forever between riches and comparative poverty — between a life of ease and a life of service.

HELEN KELLER

THE DEAF, DUMB AND BLIND GIRL
WHO WAS LIKENED TO NAPOLEON

MARK TWAIN once said: "The two most interesting characters of the nineteenth century are Napoleon and Helen Keller." When Mark Twain said that, Helen Keller was only fifteen years old. Today she still remains one of the most interesting characters.

Helen Keller is totally blind; yet she has read far more books than most people who can see. She has probably read a hundred times as many books as the average person, and she has written eleven books herself. She made a motion picture of her own life and acted in it. She is totally deaf, yet she enjoys music far more than many people who can hear.

For nine years of her life, she was deprived of the power of speech; yet she has delivered lectures in every state in the Union; for four years, she appeared as a headliner in vaudeville; and she has travelled all over Europe.

Helen Keller was born perfectly normal. For the first year and a half of her life, she could see and hear like other children and had even begun to talk. Then suddenly she was overwhelmed by catastrophe. She was struck down by an illness which left her deaf, dumb and blind at the age of nineteen months and blighted her whole existence.

She began to grow up like a wild animal in the jungle. She smashed and destroyed every object that displeased her. She crammed her food into her mouth with both hands; and when anyone tried to correct her, she flung herself upon the floor and kicked and thrashed and tried to scream.

In utter despair, her parents sent her to the Perkins Institute for the Blind in Boston, pleading for a teacher. Then, like an angel of light, Anne Mansfield Sullivan came into her tragic life. Miss Sullivan was only twenty years old when she left the Perkins Institute in Boston and undertook what seemed an impossible task—the task of educating a deaf, dumb and blind child. Her own life had been filled with tragic and heart-breaking poverty.

At the age of ten, Anne Sullivan had been sent with her little brother to live at the poorhouse in Tewksbury, Massachusetts. The poorhouse was so overcrowded that the two children slept in what was known as the "dead room"—the room where dead bodies were laid out to await burial. The little brother was sickly and after six months, he died. And Anne herself, when she was only fourteen years old, had become so nearly blind that she was sent to the Perkins Institute to learn to read with her fingers. But she did not go blind. Not then. Her sight improved. It was only a half-century later, and shortly before her death, that the darkness finally closed in upon her.

I cannot possibly make clear in a few words the miracle Anne Sullivan wrought with Helen Keller; nor how in one short month, she succeeded in communicating with a child who lived in an utter darkness and a withering silence. That story has been told unforgettably in Helen Keller's own book, *The Story of My Life*. No one who has read that book can possibly help remembering the happiness of the little deaf, dumb and blind child on the day she first realized there was such a thing as human speech. "It would have been difficult," she says, "to find a happier child than I was as I lay in my crib at the close of that eventful day and lived over the joys it had brought me, and for the first time, longed for a new day to come."

When Helen Keller was twenty years old, her education had advanced so far that she entered Radcliffe College, and her teacher went with her. By that time, she could not only read and write as well as any other student at College, but she had even regained her power of speech. The first sentence she ever learned to say was "I am not dumb now." She said it over and over again, thrilled, elated at the miracle—"I am not dumb now."

She speaks like a person who has a slight foreign accent. She writes her books and magazine articles on a typewriter that types in Braille, or raised dots. And if she wants to make corrections in the margin, she pricks little holes in the paper with a hairpin.

I have noticed that as she walks, she often talks to herself. But she doesn't move her lips as you and I do—she moves her fingers, and talks to herself in sign language. Her secretary told me that Miss Keller's sense of direction is no better than yours or mine. She often loses her way in her own home, and if the furniture is moved, she is at a complete loss. Many people expect her to have a sort of uncanny sixth sense because she is blind, yet scientific tests have shown that her sense of touch and taste and smell are just about like yours.

However, her sense of touch is so acute that she can understand what her friends are saying by placing her fingers lightly over their lips, and she enjoys music by putting her hands on the wood of a piano, or a violin; she even listens to the radio by feeling the vibrations of the cabinet. She enjoys singing by putting her fingers lightly on the throat of the singer, but she herself cannot sing or carry a tune.

If Helen Keller were to shake hands with you and then meet you and shake hands again five years later, she would remember you by your handshake — whether you were angry or happy, disappointed or gay.

She rows a boat and swims and loves to gallop through the woods on horseback. She plays checkers and chess with a set made especially for her. She even plays solitaire with a deck of cards that has raised figures; and on rainy days, she often spends the time knitting or crocheting.

Most of us think that about the worst affliction in the world is to become blind. Yet Helen Keller says she doesn't mind being blind nearly so much as being deaf. In the utter darkness and silence which separates her from the world, the thing which she misses most is the friendly sound of the human voice.

3

ANDREW CARNEGIE

HE MADE MORE MILLIONAIRES THAN
ANY MAN WHO EVER LIVED

ANDREW CARNEGIE was born without benefit of doctor or midwife because his people were too poor to afford either. He started working for two cents an hour —and he made four hundred million dollars.

Once I visited the cottage in Dunfermline, Scotland, where he was born. The house had only two rooms. His father ran a weaving business on the ground floor and the family cooked and ate and slept in one tiny, dark attic room upstairs.

When the Carnegie family came to America, Andrew's father made tablecloths and peddled them from door to door. His mother took in washing and stitched boots for a shoemaker. Andrew had only one shirt, so his mother washed and ironed that shirt every night after he had gone to bed. She worked for sixteen to eighteen hours a day, and Andrew adored her. When he was twenty-two, he promised her that he would never marry as long as she lived. And he didn't. He didn't marry until his mother died thirty years later. He was fifty-two when he married and sixty-two when his first and only child was born.

As a boy, he said to his mother over and over: "Mother, I am going to be rich some day so that you can have silk dresses and servants and a carriage of your own." He often said that he inherited all his brains from his mother, that his undying love for her was one of the driving forces of his spectacular career. When she died, his grief was so intense that he couldn't bear to speak her name for fifteen years. He once paid the mortgage on an old woman's house in Scotland merely because she looked like his mother.

Andrew Carnegie was known as the steel king; yet he knew very little about the manufacture of steel. He had hundreds, perhaps thousands, of men working for him who knew more about steel than he did. But he knew how to handle men—and that is what made him rich. Early in life, he showed a flare for organization, for leadership, for making other people work for him.

When he was a boy in Scotland, he got hold of a mother rabbit, Presto! He soon had a whole nest of little rabbits—and nothing to feed them. But he had a brilliant idea. He told the boys in the neighborhood that if they would go out and pull enough clover and dandelions to feed the rabbits, he would name the bunnies in their honor. The plan worked like magic.

Years later, Carnegie used the same psychology in business. For example, he wanted to sell steel rails to the Pennsylvania Railroad. Mr. J. Edgar Thomson was the president of the Pennsylvania Railroad at that time. So Andrew Carnegie built a huge steel mill in Pittsburgh and called it the "J. Edgar Thomson Steel Works." Naturally, Mr. Thomson was delighted, and it didn't take much persuasion to get him to order his steel rails from the company that bore his name.

Carnegie got a job as a telegraph messenger boy in Pittsburgh. The pay was fifty cents a day. It seemed like a fortune. He was a stranger in town. He was afraid he might lose his position, because he didn't know how to get about, so he memorized the names and addresses of every firm in the business section of the city. He longed to be an operator; so he studied telegraphy at night and rushed down to the office early each morning to practise on the keys.

One morning the wire was hot with big news. Philadelphia was calling Pittsburgh, calling frantically. There was no operator on duty. So Andrew Carnegie rushed to the wire, took the message, delivered it, and was immediately promoted to the position of operator with his salary doubled.

His restless energy, his sleepless ambition attracted attention. The Pennsylvania Railroad erected a telegraph line of its own. Andrew Carnegie was made operator, then private secretary to the division superintendent.

Suddenly one day an event happened that started him on the way to fortune. An inventor came and sat down beside him in a railroad train and showed him the model of a new sleeping car he had invented. The sleeping cars of that day were crude bunks nailed to the sides of freight cars. This new invention was much like the Pullman car of today. Carnegie had shrewd Scotch foresight. He saw that the invention had possibilities— enormous possibilities. So he borrowed money and bought stock in the concern. The company paid sensational dividends and when Andrew Carnegie reached twenty-five, his annual income from this one investment alone was five thousand dollars a year.

Once a wooden bridge burned on the railroad and tied up traffic for days. Andrew Carnegie was a division superintendent at the time. Wooden bridges were doomed. He saw that. Iron was the coming thing. So he borrowed money, formed a company, started building iron bridges—and the profits poured in so fast that he was almost dizzy.

This son of a weaver had the golden touch. He rode high, wide and handsome. Luck was with him, phenomenal luck. He and some friends bought a farm amidst the oil fields of Western Pennsylvania for forty thousand dollars and made a million dollars out of it in one year. By the time this canny Scot had reached twenty-seven, he had an income of a thousand dollars a week-and fifteen years before he had been working for twenty cents a day.

It was 1862 now. Abe Lincoln was in the White House. The Civil War was raging. Prices were skyrocketing. Big things were happening. Frontiers were being pushed back. The far West was opening up. Rail-roads were soon to be thrown across the continent. Cities were to be built. America trembled on the threshold of an astonishing era.

And Andy Carnegie, with the smoke and flames belching from his steel furnaces, rode up on a tidal wave of prosperity—rode and kept on riding until he had acquired riches such as had never been dreamed of before in the history of mankind.

Yet he never worked very hard. He played about

half of the time. He said that he surrounded himself with assistants who knew more than he did—and he spurred them on to pile up millions for him. He was Scotch, but he wasn't too Scotch. He let his partners share in his profits and he made more millionaires than any other man who has ever lived.

He went to school only four years in his life, but in spite of that he wrote eight books of travel, biography, essays and economics and gave away sixty million dollars to public libraries, and seventy-eight millions for the advancement of education.

He memorized all the poems that Bobbie Burns ever wrote; and he could repeat from memory all of *Macbeth*, all of *Hamlet*, all of *King Lear, Romeo and Juliet*, and all of *The Merchant of Venice*.

He was not a member of any church, but he gave away more than seven thousand pipe organs to churches.

He gave away three hundred and sixty-five

million dollars. That means he gave away a million dollars for every day in the year. Newspapers ran contests and offered prizes to those who could best tell him how to give away his hoard of gold. For he declared it was a disgrace to die rich.

JOHN D. ROCKEFELLER

SHE TURNED HIM DOWN BECAUSE
HE HAD "NO PROSPECTS" —HIS NAME WAS JOHN D.!

JOHN D. ROCKEFELLER did three astonishing things:

First, he amassed probably the greatest fortune in all history. He started out in life hoeing potatoes under the boiling sun for four cents an hour. In those days, there were not half a dozen men in all the United States who were worth even one million dollars; but John D. managed to amass a fortune estimated at anywhere from one billion to two billion dollars.

And yet the first girl he fell in love with refused to marry him. Why? Because her mother said she was not going to let a daughter of hers "throw herself away" on a man who had such poor prospects as John D. Rockefeller.

The second astonishing thing that Mr. Rockefeller did was this: he gave away $750,000,000, more money than anyone else has done in all history.

And the third astonishing thing about Rockefeller was that he lived to be ninety-seven. He was one of the most bitterly hated men in America. He received thousands of letters from people threatening to kill him. He had to be protected day and night by armed bodyguards. He endured the terrific nervous and physical strain of building up and managing all his far-flung enterprises.

The strain of business killed Harriman, the railroad builder, at sixty-one.

Woolworth founded his vast chain of five-and-ten-cent stores and was done with life at sixty-seven.

"Buck" Duke made a hundred million dollars out of tobacco and died at sixty-eight.

But John D. Rockefeller made a far greater fortune than Woolworth, Duke and Harriman all put together. And remember, only thirty white men in a million ever reach the age of ninety-seven—and there is probably not one man in a hundred million who ever reaches ninety-seven without needing artificial teeth. But John D. at ninety-seven hadn't a false tooth in his head.

What was the secret of his long life? He probably inherited a tendency to live long. And this tendency was strengthened by a calm, placid disposition. He never got excited and he was never rushed.

When he was head of the Standard Oil Company, he had a couch in his office at 26 Broadway; and come what might, he had a half-hour's nap everyday at noon. And he continued to take five naps a day until his death.

When John D. Rockefeller was fifty-five, he had a physical breakdown. That was one of the happiest accidents that ever happened in the whole history of medicine; for because of his own illness, John D. was stimulated to give millions to medical research. As a result of his ill health, the Rockefeller Foundation is spending almost a million dollars a month to promote health throughout the world.

I was in China during the terrible cholera epidemic of 1932, and in the midst of all that poverty and ignorance and disease I was able to walk into the Rockefeller Medical College at Peking and get a vaccination for cholera. Never until then had I realised how much Rockefeller was doing for suffering humanity in Asia and the remote corners of the earth. The Rockefeller Foundation has tried to stamp out hookworm all over the world; it is waging a winning battle against malaria; and its physicians discovered a vaccine for the dreaded yellow fever.

John D. earned his first dollar by helping his mother raise turkeys and until his death he kept a flock of fine turkeys on his eight thousand acre estate—kept them to remind him of the scenes of his childhood.

He saved all the nickels his mother paid him for tending turkeys and stored the money in a cracked teacup which he kept on the mantel piece. He worked on a farm for thirty-seven cents a day and saved all his wages until he accumulated fifty dollars. Then he lent those fifty dollars to his employer at seven per cent interest and discovered that his fifty dollars could make as much for him in a year as he could earn by ten days of gruelling work.

"That settled it," he said. "I determined then and there to let money be my slave instead of being the slave of money."

John D. didn't spoil his son with too much money. For example, he gave him a penny for each fence post he could find on the estate that needed to be repaired. He found thirteen in one day, and was paid thirteen cents. Then John D. paid his son fifteen cents an hour for repairing fences, and his mother gave him five cents an hour for practising on the violin.

John D. never went to college. He finished high school and attended a commercial school for a few months. He was through with academic study forever when he was sixteen; yet he gave fifty million dollars to the University of Chicago.

He was always intensely interested in the church. As a young man he taught Sunday school classes, never danced, never played cards, never went to the theatre and didn't smoke and didn't drink.

He said grace before each meal and he had the

Bible read to him daily—and in addition, he also had read to him selections from a book of poems and prayers containing uplift messages for every day.

The Rockefeller fortune is still growing at the approximate rate of one hundred dollars a minute, yet Mr. Rockefeller's only great ambition was to round out a century of life; and he said that if he were alive on his hundredth birthday—July 8, 1939—he was going to lead a band on his estate at Pocantico Hills. And the tune they were going to play was: *When You and I Were Young, Maggie*.

FLORENZ ZIEGFELD

HE KNEW THE TELEPHONE NUMBERS OF
MORE BEAUTIFUL GIRLS THAN
ANY MAN IN HISTORY

◦─ FOR TWENTY-FOUR YEARS, the *Ziegfeld Follies* blazed supreme over the firmament of Broadway. No other revue in the entire world was ever staged so lavishly or acclaimed with such roars of delight. No other revue ever made so much money, and no other revue ever lost so much money.

Florenz Ziegfeld knew the telephone numbers of more beautiful girls than any other man living. In his Blue Book of Beauty were listed the names, addresses, and telephone numbers of thousands of glamorous girls. Fifty or sixty aspiring young Venuses paraded before his critical glance every day.

He was proud of the fact that he was called the Glorifier of the American Girl. It was a title richly deserved. He often took some drab little girl no one had ever looked at twice and transformed her on the stage into a dazzling creature of mystery and seduction. Form and grace—these alone—were the covered passport to the Ziegfeld stage. The glamor was supplied by Ziegfeld himself.

Ziegfeld was as regal in his extravagance as an Oriental potentate. He squandered millions of dollars on costumes, combing the markets of Europe and India and Asia for the most beautiful fabrics money could buy. Even the *linings* of dresses had to be of the finest silk, for he claimed no woman could feel really beautiful unless she had beautiful cloth against her skin.

In order to get just the proper hats for a certain cow-boy number he had in mind, he postponed the production of *Show Boat* for three entire months. Once, after he had spent a quarter of a million dollars on a production, he closed it after one performance, because he felt it was unworthy of the glorious Ziegfeld tradition.

He did everything on a lavish scale. Although he communicated with hundreds of people daily, he never troubled to dictate a letter. Telegrams and cables fluttered in his wake like autumn leaves in a gale of wind. Wherever he went, he carried with him a telegraph blank. He used to get on the train at Grand Central Station and use up a whole pad of telegraph blanks before he reached 125th Street.

Incredible as it seems, he actually sat in the orchestra pit during rehearsals and sent telegrams to the actors across the footlights. He sent telegrams to people who were within range of his voice. He once leaned out of his window and yelled at the man in the window opposite: "Say, I sent you a telegram. Why haven't you answered it?"

It was almost impossible for him to walk past a telephone booth without stopping to call up a dozen people; and he got out of bed almost every morning at six o'clock in order to telephone to his staff.

He could scheme for hours to save seventeen or eighteen dollars; and the next day, he'd drop a hundred thousand dollars in Wall Street without batting an eye. He once borrowed five thousand dollars from Ed Wynn, and spent that five thousand dollars of borrowed money to hire a private train to carry him across the continent.

He made women feel beautiful by the sheer power of his chivalry and consideration. On opening night, every girl in his chorus received a box of flowers from him. Even old and half-demented women who applied to him for jobs were treated with the same consideration he showed to all the rest.

He paid his most famous stars an average of $5,000 a week; often, at the end of the season they had more money in the bank than he himself had.

When he started in the show business, chorus girls were getting $30 a week; but under his profligate reign, feminine pulchritude reached a market price of $125 a week.

Ziegfeld's first venture into show business was made at the precocious age of fourteen. Running away from home, he became a trick rider and fancy shooter in Buffalo Bill's Wild West Show.

At the age of twenty-five, he was cleaning up a fortune as manager to Sandow, the husky strong man of the naughty Nineties.

Two years later, he was in London—broke—without a shilling to his name. He'd staked his luck at Monte Carlo, and with a turn of the wheel, he had lost his shirt.

Being penniless never worried this great entrepreneur. By the sheer witchery of his manner, he got together another show and sailed back in triumph to America with the most sensational star in Europe—the vivacious, scintillating, and palpitating Anna Held—the Mae West of her day.

The most canny producers in America had been cabling and pleading with Anna Held to come to New York. They had tempted her with extravagant offers. Yet it was Florenz Ziegfeld, only twenty-seven years old, practically unknown, and without a dime in his pocket, who walked into her dressing room, charmed her, got her name on a contract, and started skyrocketing to fame.

Anna Held was an immediate sensation. She took America by storm. Corsets, face powder, hats, perfumes, horses, cocktails, puppies, and cigars were named in her honor. She was toasted in champagne from coast to coast. And within a year,

Florenz Ziegfeld married her.

Many years later, after he had divorced Anna Held, he fell ecstatically in love with Billie Burke. The very day after he met her, he bought out an entire flower shop and sent the complete stock to her home—sent her everything from sweet peas and orchids and carnations to the orange trees in the window. And when Billie Burke told him that she had tried to thank him by telephone, but had not been able to because his line was busy, he had a golden phone installed, with a special ring, for her private use.

Ziegfeld loved indecision. He hated to make up his mind. He used to keep a box of licorice drops on his desk; and when a friend asked him if he really liked licorice, he said: "I'll tell you why I eat them. They're all black, so I don't have to make up my mind which color I like best."

He hired the most famous comedians in the world

for his Follies; but he himself never laughed at their antics. Neither Ed Wynn nor Eddie Cantor nor Will Rogers could make him crack a smile. He was so cool that his actors gave him the nickname of "Ice Water."

For twenty-four years, the opening night of the Follies was something of an event in roaring old New York. Limousines jammed the street; silk hats and ermine wraps thronged the lobby; and sharp-witted speculators made tired business men pay as high as $300 for a pair of seats in the front row. Backstage was filled with clamor and tumult. Wardrobe mistresses and messenger boys bumped into each other; comedians with stage fright muttered in the wings; and chorus girls hunted frantically for clothes. In the mad whirl, there was only one man who remained calm; cool and composed—that man was Ziegfeld. New York's sophisticated first nighters put on their tails and white ties for the auspicious occasion; but Ziegfeld himself appeared in a plain gray business suit. He didn't even allow himself the luxury of a seat. He watched the show from the stairs that led to the balcony.

When Wall Street crashed in 1929, it was lights and final curtain for the career of Ziegfeld the great Glorifier. From then on, the magician who had lavished millions on tinsel and glitter for the gayest pageant in the world, could hardly raise the money to pay his rent. The last Follies was staged with funds partly supplied by his own stars and employees.

Ziegfeld died in 1932 in California, and as he slipped into the delirium of death, he imagined he was directing a revue. His stage was a white hospital room, his orchestra was only a radio; and for a stage crew, he had nothing but his terrified valet. His lips were parched, and his eyes were glowing with fever, but he sat up in bed and shouted his directions to an invisible cast.

"Curtain!" he cried. "Fast music! Lights! Ready for the last finale!" And finally he murmured: "Great! The show looks good.... The show.... looks.... good."

ENRICO CARUSO

HIS PEASANT MOTHER WENT BAREFOOT
TO PAY FOR HIS MUSIC LESSONS AND
HE BECAME THE GREATEST SINGER IN THE WORLD

WHEN ENRICO CARUSO died in 1921, at the age of 48, entire nations were struck dumb with sorrow; for the most beautiful voice in the memory of living men was still and silent forever. Caruso was snatched away from life while the plaudits of the world were ringing in his ears. Exhausted from overwork, he caught a common cold, neglected it, and for six months battled valiantly with death while the world that loved him sang masses, and sent a million fervent prayers winging their way up towards the inscrutable gates of destiny. Caruso's magical voice was not merely a gift from the gods, it was the reward of long years of exhausting work—of patient practice and unflagging determination.

In the beginning, his voice was so light and thin that one teacher told him: "You can't sing. You haven't any voice at all. It sounds like the wind in the shutters."

For years, his voice cracked on high notes, and his acting was so poor that he was actually hissed during a performance. Few men have ever drunk so deeply of the heady wine of success as the immortal Caruso; yet at the very high noon of his fame, when he remembered the ordeal of those early years, he would burst into tears.

His mother died when he was fifteen, and all his life he carried her portrait with him wherever he went. She had given birth to twenty-one children.

Eighteen of them died in infancy. Only three of them lived. She was merely a peasant woman who had known little else but hardship and sorrow; yet somehow, she sensed that this one son was hallowed by the fire of genius, and no sacrifice was too great for her to make. Caruso used to say, "My mother went without shoes in order that I might sing." And he wept as he said it.

When he was only ten years old, his father took him out of school and put him to work in a factory. Every evening after work, Caruso studied music, but he was twenty-one years old before he was able to sing himself out of the factory.

In those days, he jumped at the chance to sing for his supper in a neighborhood café. He frequently hired himself out to warble serenades beneath some lady's window. While the lady's tone-deaf lover stood out boldly in the moonlight going through all the gestures of adoration, Caruso, hidden in the doorway, would pour forth his soul in tones as mellow and seductive as Apollo's.

Finally, when he got his first real chance to sing in opera, he was so nervous at rehearsal that his voice broke and splintered like falling glass. Again and again he tried, but every note was a disaster. At last he burst into tears and fled from the theatre.

When he actually made his debut in opera, he was tipsy. He was so tipsy that the audience drowned out his voice with hoots and catcalls. In those days, he was only an understudy. One evening the tenor who sang the leading role was suddenly taken ill. Caruso was absent. Messengers were sent dashing through the streets to find him. Finally he was discovered in a wine shop, about three sheets to the wind. He ran as fast as he could to the theatre. When he arrived there breathless with excitement, the heat of the stuffy dressing room and the wine of the grape were too much. Suddenly the whole world began to spin like a merry-go-round. And when Caruso walked on to the stage, pandemonium broke loose in the theatre.

At the end of that performance, he was fired. The next day he was so heartbroken, so desperate, that he made up his mind to commit suicide.

He had in his pocket only one lira—just enough to buy a bottle of wine. He had had no food all day. And just as he was drinking his wine and planning how to kill himself, the door flew open and in dashed a messenger—a messenger from the opera.

"Caruso!" he shouted. "Caruso, come! The people won't listen to that other tenor. They hissed him off the stage. They're shouting for you! For you!"

"For me!" Caruso cried. "That's silly. Why, they don't even know my name."

"Of course they don't know it," the messenger panted. "But they want you just the same. They're shouting for 'that drunkard'!"

When Enrico Caruso died, he was several times a millionaire. His phonograph records alone earned him over two million dollars. Yet he had been so seared by the poverty of his youth, that up to the end of his life he wrote down every expenditure in a little book. Regardless of whether he bought a priceless bit of old lace or carved ivory for his collections, or tipped a bellboy, he made a note of the exact amount.

He was haunted by all the superstitions of the Italian peasantry. To the day of his death, he feared the Evil Eye. He never crossed the ocean without first consulting an astrologer. He never walked under a ladder, or wore a new suit on Friday. And nothing could induce him to begin a journey or start a new undertaking on Tuesday or Friday.

He had a veritable mania for cleanliness, and he changed his clothing—everything from underwear to spats—whenever he came into the house.

He possessed the rarest and most valuable voice in the world, yet he smoked in his dressing-room while he was putting on his make-up. When people asked him if smoking wouldn't hurt his voice, he merely laughed. He scoffed at dieting; and at every performance, just before he stepped on to the stage, he took a nip of whiskey and soda to clear his throat.

He had left school when he was ten, and he practically never read a book. He said to his wife: "Why should I read? I study from life itself."

Instead of reading, he spent hours over his collection of stamps and rare coins. He had an extraordinary gift for caricature, and every week he contributed a cartoon to an Italian periodical.

For years he suffered from excruciating headaches that tortured his senses and made him scream from pain. As he grew older, his astonishing vitality began to wane. He spent more and more of his time in the quiet of his study and cared less and less for the plaudits of the throng. Finally he succumbed to a brooding melancholy and spent hours poring over his newspaper clippings, cutting them out and trimming them and pasting them in his book of memories.

He was born in Naples. But when he first tried to sing in his home town, the papers criticized him and the audience was cold, and unresponsive. Caruso was deeply hurt and never forgave them. In the heyday of his glory, he often went back to Naples, but he bitterly refused ever to sing there again.

Perhaps the greatest and happiest moment of his life was when he first held his daughter Gloria in his arms. He said over and over again that he was only waiting for the moment when she would be big enough to run down the corridor and open the door of his studio. And one day in Italy, as Caruso stood by his piano, that very thing happened. He caught the little girl up in his arms, and with tears in his eyes, he said to his wife: "Do you remember—I was just waiting for this moment to come?"

And within a week he was dead.

CAPTAIN ROBERT FALCON SCOTT

"HE SOUGHT THE SECRETS OF THE POLE—
HE FOUND THE SECRETS OF GOD"

I KNOW of no story more heroic, more inspiring, or more tragic than that of Captain Robert Falcon Scott, the second man to reach the South Pole. The tale of how Scott and two companions met tragic death on the Ross Ice Barrier still has the power to sway mankind.

The news of Scott's death reached England on a sunny afternoon in February, 1913. Crocuses were blooming in Regent Park. England was stunned as nothing else has stunned her since Nelson's death at Trafalgar.

Twenty-two years later, England dedicated a final memorial to Scott—a polar museum, the first polar museum in the world. Arctic explorers from all over the earth gathered at its dedication. Across the front of the building runs a Latin inscription of Robert Scott. It says: "He sought the secrets of the Pole. He found the secrets of God."

Scott began his tragic dash for the South Pole in the *Terra Nova,* and from the moment the ship nosed her way into the icy waters of the Circle, he was beset and bedevilled by bad luck.

Enormous waves battered the hull. Cargo was swept from the deck. Tons of sea water thundered down into the hold. The boiler fires were swamped. The pumps were clogged. And for days the gallant ship rolled helplessly in the trough of the smashing seas.

But Scott's bad luck had only begun.

He brought along tough little ponies that had been hardened to cold on the frozen tundras of Siberia, but they suffered agonies. They floundered helplessly in the powdery snow; they broke their legs in treacherous crevasses and had to be shot.

The dogs too—veteran huskies from the Yukon— went wild and dashed blindly over the edges of the glacier cracks.

Then Scott and his four companions made the final dash for the Pole, alone, harnessed to a sledge that weighed a thousand pounds. Day after day they slogged over fields of rough ice, each man pulling, gasping and choking in the thin frigid air nine thousand feet above sea level.

Yet they did not complain. At the end of the cruelest journey ever undertaken by man lay victory, lay the mysterious Pole, undisturbed since the Six Days of Creation—the Pole where nothing lives nor breathes, nor stirs—not even a wandering gull.

And on the fourteenth day they reached the Pole — *but* — only to find consternation and heartbreak. Before them, at the top of a stick, a tattered piece of cloth flaunted triumphantly in the bitter wind. A flag—the flag of Norway! Amundsen, the Norwegian had been there before them!—and they realized that after years of preparation, after months of torment, they had been cheated of victory by five short weeks.

Crushed with disappointment they started home.

The story of their tragic struggle back toward civilization is an Odyssey of suffering. The stinging blasts coated their features with ice and froze their very beards. They stumbled and fell, and every injury brought them a step nearer death. First, Petty Officer Evans, the strongest man in the outfit, slipped and crashed his skull against the ice, and died.

Then Captain Oates fell ill. His feet were frostbitten. He could hardly walk. He knew he was holding his companions back. So one night Oates did a godlike thing. He walked out into a raging blizzard to die in order that others might live.

Without heroics, without melodrama, he calmly announced: "I'm going outside. I may be gone some time." He was gone forever. His frozen body was never found. But today a monument stands on the spot of his disappearance, and it reads: "Hereabouts died a very gallant gentleman."

Scott and his two companions staggered on. They no longer looked like men. Their noses, their fingers, their feet were brittle with cold. And on the nineteenth of February, 1912, fifty days after they had left the Pole, they pitched camp for the last time. They had fuel enough to make two cups of tea apiece, and enough food to keep them alive for two more days. They thought they were saved—they were only eleven miles away from a depot of buried supplies. With one terrible march they could make it.

Suddenly they were overwhelmed with tragedy.

Down over the rim of the earth roared a howling blizzard, a fury of wind so fierce, so sharp that it cut ridges in the ice. No creature on earth could face it and live. Scott and his men were held prisoners in their tent for eleven days while the blizzard raged and snarled. Their supplies were exhausted. It was the end and they knew it.

There was a way out—an easy way out. They had opium, a large quantity of opium brought along for just such an emergency. A big dose of that and they could all lie down to pleasant dreams, never to wake again.

But they ignored the drug. They resolved to face death with the fine sportsmanship characteristic of old England.

During the last hour of his life Scott wrote a letter to Sir James Barrie, describing the end. Their food was gone. Death was almost upon them. Yet Scott writes: "It would do your heart good if you could hear us fill our tent with ringing songs of cheer."

One day eight months later when the Antarctic sun shone peacefully over the gleaming ice, their frozen bodies were found by a searching party.

They were buried where they perished—buried under a cross made of two skiis lashed together. And over their common grave were written these beautiful words from Tennyson:

One equal temper of heroic hearts
Made weak by time and fate but strong in will
To strive, to seek, to find, but not to yield.

LAWRENCE TIBBETT

HE ONCE PICKED GRAPES TO PAY HIS
RENT—TODAY HIS VOICE IS WORTH A FORTUNE

IN 1922, Lawrence Tibbett was living near Los Angeles having a hard time trying to support his wife. He sang in a church choir on Sunday, and picked up five dollars now and then by singing *Oh, Promise Me!* at a wedding.

He had studied for years; but he wasn't getting anywhere. However, he had a friend, Rupert Hughes, who believed in him. Hughes said: "You have the makings of a great voice. You ought to study in New York."

That little bit of friendly encouragement proved to be the turning point in Tibbett's life, for it caused him to borrow twenty-five hundred dollars and start East. What if he failed to make good in New York? Well, if he did, he was determined to go back to California and make a living selling automobile trucks.

That was in 1922. Lawrence Tibbett was so poor he couldn't afford to live in town.... So he rented a house in the country. Fortunately, the house stood in the middle of a vineyard; he got all the grapes he wanted to eat free; and he confessed that there were times when he had very little to eat except grapes. The house cost him only twelve dollars and fifty cents a month; but little as that was, it was sometimes more than he could make as a singer. He once got ten months behind in his rent and had to pick grapes and prune vines to pay off his debt.

He rented a piano for five dollars a month, but he couldn't put it in the front room because the rickety old house stood on a steep hillside and the front part of it was propped up on high stilts and he was afraid the piano would fall through the floor and go rolling and bouncing through the grape vines until it struck the bottom of the hill.

When he first came to New York, he couldn't afford to buy even the cheapest seat in the Metropolitan Opera House. So he used to pay two dollars and twenty cents for the privilege of standing up in the back of the mighty Metropolitan Opera House to listen to the glamorous performances of the immortal Scotti and the beautiful Mary Garden. In those days, he had to borrow money from his friends to pay for his room rent and music lessons.

Yet ten years later, he himself was striding across the proud stage of the Metropolitan, arousing a frenzy of wild huzzas, winning twenty-two curtain calls at a single performance and making himself one of the most famous baritones in all the world.

Every year there are hundreds of ambitious youngsters with good voices who flock to New York, eager to win fame and fortune. I have often wondered how many of them fail to rise above mediocrity.

I asked Lawrence Tibbett, and he said about nine hundred and ninety-nine out of every thousand; he added that the majority of them didn't fail because they lacked good voices, but because they lacked vocal intelligence. They failed, he said, because they had no gift for showmanship, no ability to grip their audience, to put their songs over, and make people feel what they were singing.

Lawrence Tibbett spent his childhood in Bakersfield, California. For years, his father had been a cowboy in California, riding the range, repairing fences, branding calves and battling with cattle rustlers. The old man carried a big pearl-handled revolver in his belt; he was a dead shot. He had two notches in his gun, because he had already killed two cattle thieves, and now he was sheriff of Kern County, California. He had a regular arsenal of guns in the house, and kept a huge blood-hound, with long ears and sad eyes, chained up in the back yard. Whenever a shooting occurred, the phone would ring and Sheriff Tibbett would grab his dog and gun, dash away to the scene of the crime, and put the bloodhound on the trail, and Rod—that was the old bloodhound's name—Rod would go bellowing across fields and through orchards and Sheriff Tibbett would run behind, holding on to the leash, waving his arms and crying: "Rod's got him this time. Rod's got him." But, instead of catching the criminal, Rod usually tracked down an old cow or a coyote.

Being a sheriff seemed like a mighty exciting and

glamorous business to young Larry Tibbett, so his boyhood ambition was to be a sheriff himself like his father.

Then suddenly a dramatic and tragic thing happened. His father was shot and killed in a battle with Jim Mc-Kinney, one of the most notorious bank robbers and gun men of the West.

That shooting changed the whole course of Lawrence Tibbett's life, for his father was a very religious man, bitterly opposed to smoking and dancing and card playing and the theatre; and Tibbett told me that if his father had not been shot, he himself would never have dared to become a singer and an actor.

As a boy in high school, Tibbett developed an inferiority complex. His mother ran a rooming house. He had only one suit of clothes, his trousers were too short, and he couldn't buy his best girl an ice cream soda at the corner drug store. The other students snubbed him and paid no attention to him. So he resolved to make a name for himself, and he looked about for a short cut to distinction. He tried to become a member of the glee club—and they wouldn't have him. He tried to get a part in the high school plays.... and no one wanted him. This boy who was destined to become the most famous singer that ever came out of California was turned down cold when he wanted to sing in a high school concert. The spark of genius didn't shine through his voice until he was twenty-one years old.

Tibbett says that the greatest music is that which thrills you most and that a lot of our popular music is good, very good.

The End of a Perfect Day is one of the most popular songs ever written. At least five million people bought copies of it, and Lawrence Tibbett says that that humble song is a truly great one.

He believes that *Old Man River* and *The*

Rhapsody in Blue are as fine as anything ever written by the greatest Viennese composers that ever lived.

WILLIAM SHAKESPEARE

SHAKESPEARE HAD A SHOT-GUN WEDDING

◦◦ NO ONE paid much attention to him while he lived. A hundred years after his death his name was still practically unknown. Yet since that time millions of words have been written about him; he has aroused more comment than any other writer who ever sharpened his wisdom teeth on a goose-quill pen; and thousands of people, every year, make pilgrimage to the place where he was born.

I, for one, was there in 1921. I used to wander

cross-country from Stratford to Slattery—treading the fields swept by his eager feet when, as an awkward country boy, he hurried to keep tryst with his sweetheart, Anne Whately.

Little did William Shakespeare suspect then that his name would ring down the centuries in a paean of glory. And, fortunately, little did he suspect that his idyllic young love was doomed to sorrow—and to years of regret.

For there is no doubt about it—the tragedy of Shakespeare's life was his marriage. True, he loved Anne Whately—but late of moonlight nights he had been tempting fate with another lass, Anne Hathaway. When Anne Hathaway learned that her lover had taken out a license to wed someone else, she was stunned—she was crazed with fear. In desperation she rushed to the homes of her neighbors, and weeping with shame, explained why Shakespeare would have to marry her. Her neighbors—simple, honest-hearted yeomen—bristled with moral indignation. The very next day, they hurried to the town hall, and posted a bond for the marriage of Shakespeare to Anne Hathaway.

Shakespeare's bride was eight years older than himself—and from the very start, their marriage was a miserable farce. Time and again in his plays, he warns men against marrying older women—and as a matter of fact, he lived with Anne Hathaway very little of the time. Most of his married life was passed in London, and he probably returned to his family no oftener than once a year.

Today, Stratford-on-Avon is one of the loveliest towns in England—little thatched cottages, gardens of hollyhocks, quaint winding streets. But when Shakespeare lived there? It was dirty, poverty-stricken, and devastated by disease. There were no sewers. Pigs swarmed through the main streets devouring the garbage; and Shakespeare's father, one of the town officials, was fined for hoarding, outside his door, a pile of refuse from the stable.

We, in America, think we have had hard times, but in Shakespeare's day, one half the population of Stratford was living on public relief. Most of the people were illiterate. Neither Shakespeare's father nor mother nor sister nor daughter nor granddaughter could either read or write.

The man who was destined to become the power and the glory of English literature, had to leave school when he was thirteen and go to work. His father was a glove-maker and a farmer—and Shakespeare milked cows, sheared the sheep, churned the butter, and helped tan leather and soften hides.

But when he died, Shakespeare was a wealthy man by the standards of his day. Within five years of his arrival in London, he was making good money as an actor. He bought shares in two theatres, he dabbled in real estate, he lent money at a high rate of interest, and presently his income was three hundred pounds a year. The purchasing power of money then was about twelve times what it is today—so that when Shakespeare was forty-five, he had an income of something like $20,000 a year.

Yet how much money do you imagine he left his wife in his will? Not a cent. He left her nothing whatever except his second-best bedstead; and even that was an afterthought, for he wrote it in between the lines after the will had been drawn up.

Shakespeare had been dead seven years before all his plays were published in book form. Yet shakespeare himself probably never got the equivalent of even six hundred dollars for such plays as *Hamlet, Macbeth,* or *A Midsummer Nights Dream*.

I once asked Doctor S. A. Tannenbaum, who has written a number of books on Shakespeare, if there was proof absolute that William Shakespeare of

Stratford-on-Avon wrote Shakespeare's plays. And he answered that we are as certain of that as we are that Lincoln spoke at Gettysburg. Yet many people claim that Shakespeare didn't even exist, and dozens of books have been written to prove that his plays were really the work of Sir Francis Bacon, or the Earl of Oxford.

I have often stood in front of Shakespeare's grave, gazing down at that weirdest of all epitaphs:

> *Good frend for Iesus sake forbeare,*
> *To digg the dust enclosed here;*
> *Bleste be ye man yt spares thes stones*
> *And curst be he yt moves my bones.*

He was buried in front of the pulpit in the little village church; and why was he granted this place of honor? For his genius, which men still love these four hundred years later? Hardly. The poet who was destined to be the polestar of English literature was buried in the church because he lent money to his home town. If the man who created the character of Shylock hadn't lent money to his home town, his bones would today be forgotten in an unmarked grave.

CHARLES DICKENS

HE WENT TO SCHOOL FOR ONLY FOUR
YEARS—YET HE WROTE SEVENTEEN IMMORTAL NOVELS

⁓ IN 1843, and just about Christmas time, a little book was published in London—a story destined to become immortal.

Many people have called it "the greatest little book in the world." When it first appeared, friends meeting each other on the Strand of Pall Mall asked, "Have you read it?" and the answer invariably was, "Yes, God bless him, I have."

The day it was published a thousand copies were

sold. Within a fortnight, the presses had dashed off fifteen thousand copies. Since then, it has been whirled into countless editions and has been translated into almost every language under heaven.

What is this world-famous book? Charles Dickens' *Christmas Carol*.

Charles Dickens was destined to become the most prolific and best-loved author in English literature; yet when he first started writing, he was so afraid of being laughed at that he sneaked out and mailed his first manuscript in the dead of night so that nobody would discover his audacity.

He was twenty-two years old then, and when his story was actually printed, he was so overjoyed that he wandered aimlessly around the streets with the tears streaming down his face.

He wasn't paid a cent for that story. And his next eight stories netted him—how much do you suppose? Nothing. Absolutely zero.

When he finally did get paid real money for a story, he received a check for the royal sum of five dollars. Yes, his first story brought him only five dollars; but his last manuscript brought his estate fifteen dollars a word—the highest price ever paid to an author since the beginning of time! Fifteen dollars a word! Why that is precisely fifteen times as much as Calvin Coolidge and Theodore Roosevelt were ever paid.

Most authors are ignored and forgotten within five years after their death. But sixty-three years after Dickens' death, publishers paid his estate more than a fifth of a million dollars for the story of our Lord—a little book that Dickens had written for his own children.

Charles Dickens never went to school more than foul years in all his life; yet he wrote seventeen of the greatest novels in the English language. His parents ran a school but he never went to it. Why?

Because it was a school for young ladies. Or at least, it was supposed to be. A brass plate bearing the words, "Mrs. Dickens' Establishment," hung outside the front door for a whole year; but in the whole of London, there was not even one young lady who came there to be educated.

The bills kept mounting and soaring. The creditors pleaded and swore and pounded the table. Finally, in a fit of holy indignation, they had Dickens' father flung into jail for debt.

Charles Dickens' childhood was sordid and pathetic. It was more than that—It was tragic. He was only ten years old when his father was thrown into prison, and the family had nothing to eat; so every morning, Charles went to the pawnshop and sold some of the few remaining pieces of household furniture.

He even had to sell his dearly beloved books—ten of them—the only companions he had really ever known. In later years he said, "When I sold my books, I thought my heart would break."

Finally Mrs. Dickens took four of her children and went to live with her husband in prison. At sun-up, Charles went to the prison and spent the whole day there with his family. And at night, he tramped back to the dismal attic room where he slept with two other boys—gutter-snipes from the slums of London.

They made his life a veritable hell. Finally he got a job pasting labels on bottles of blacking in a rat-infested warehouse. With the first few pennies he earned, he rented another room, a dark little hole in an attic with a heap of dirty bedding flung in the corner; yet Dickens said that little hole in an attic was "like a Paradise" to him.

In later years, Dickens, the writer, avenged his own childhood by creating the unforgettable portrait of *Oliver Twist* holding out his empty porridge bowl and asking for more.

Dickens wrote vivid scenes of perfect domestic bliss. Yet his own marriage was a failure—a dismal, tragic failure. He lived for twenty-three years with a wife he didn't love. She bore him ten children. But year by year his misery deepened. He had the whole world fawning at his feet; but his own home was filled with heartbreak.

Finally the misery became so sharp, so poignant, that he could no longer endure it. So he did an unheard-of thing in those Victorian days—he published an announcement in his own magazine declaring that he and his wife had separated. Did he shoulder the blame himself? He did not. He tried to throw it all on her.

Dickens was considered the soul of generosity. When he died, he left a fifth of a million dollars to his sister-in-law, but how much did he leave to the mother of his own children? Thirty-five dollars a week!

He was as vain as a Siamese peacock. The slightest word of criticism sent him into a towering rage. He was proud of his striking appearance and when he first came to America in 1842, he dazzled the populace with his scarlet vests and robins'-egg-blue overcoats. He shocked Americans by combing his hair in public, and Americans shocked and horrified him by letting their pigs run loose around the streets of New York City.

Dickens was the best-loved and most idolized man of his day. On his second visit to America, people stood in line for hours, shivering in the wind, while waiting to buy tickets. In Brooklyn, people lighted bonfires and lay all night on mattresses in the street, risking frost-bite and pneumonia for the privilege of paying three dollars apiece to hear him talk. And when the tickets were sold out and hundreds had to be turned away, his admirers actually started a riot.

The history of literature is packed with contradictory characters, but taken all in all, Charles Dickens is about the most astonishing of the lot.

MARK TWAIN

HE REFUSED TO INVEST MONEY
IN A NEWFANGLED CONTRAPTION CALLED THE TELEPHONE

⁓ HOLLYWOOD spent two million dollars making a film telling the life story of one of the most remarkable men this nation ever produced. He was the most famous literary figure of his generation, and became the most widely read humorous writer of all time.

He attended a log cabin school until he was twelve years old. That was all the formal education he ever had; yet Oxford and Yale Universities gave him honorary degrees, and his companionship was sought by the most learned men on earth. He made millions and millions of dollars by writing books. In fact, the products of his pen have probably made more money than those of any other writer who ever lived. Although he died many years ago, book royalties and motion picture and radio rights are still pouring a golden flood of dollars into the exchequer of his estate.

This author's real name was Samuel Langhorne Clemens, but he is known to the world as Mark Twain.

Mark Twain's entire life was an adventure. He lived through one of the most picturesque and colorful periods of American history. He was born in 1835 in a sleepy little Missouri village not far from the Mississippi River—just seven years after the first railway had been built in America; while Abe Lincoln was yet a barefoot farm laborer, walking behind a wooden plow and a team of oxen.

Mark Twain lived seventy-five thrilling years and died in Connecticut in 1910. He wrote twenty-three books. Some of them are already forgotten, but two of his books—*Huckleberry Finn* and *Tom Sawyer*—will probably achieve literary immortality and be read and treasured throughout the centuries, as long as boys are boys. These two books were written out of his own experiences. They weren't exactly written—they exploded from him.

Mark Twain was born in a tiny two-room cabin in Florida, Missouri. Today an up-to-date farmer wouldn't keep even his cows or chickens in the sort of hovel in which Mark Twain lived as a child. Eight people lived in those two dark rooms—the family of seven and a slave girl. Mark Twain was a delicate baby, so sickly that he was not expected to pull through the first winter. As he grew older, Mark Twain became quite a problem. His mother said that he gave her more trouble than all the rest of the family put together. He was always playing practical jokes. He was so bored with school that he sometimes ran away from home, and he always ran toward Old Man River. He was charmed by the mighty Mississippi, with its mysterious islands, its slow-moving rafts, its stately current swinging to the sea. He would sit beside the river for hours and dream. He was nearly drowned nine different times. But while playing Indian and pirates, exploring caves, eating turtle eggs, and drifting down the river on a raft, he was getting the priceless experiences for the scenes and characters that he was to immortalize later in his two most famous books.

Mark Twain inherited his genius for humor from his mother. He once declared that he never saw his father smile; but in speaking of his mother, he said: "She had a sort of ability which is rare in man and almost never found in woman—the ability to say a humorous thing with the perfect air of not knowing it to be humorous." That ability, inherited from her, made Mark Twain one of the most humorous public speakers who ever lived. It enabled him to make a fortune on the public platform. His mother, by the way, was so tender-hearted that she literally refused to kill flies, and even punished the cats for killing mice. She once had to drown some unwanted kittens; but she warmed the water so they would die comfortably.

Mark Twain always despised school. It deprived him of his liberty; it kept him cooped up inside four walls of a log cabin when his heart's desire was to roam the woods and explore the banks of the mysterious Mississippi.

When he was twelve, his chance to escape from the hated confinement of school came as a result of the death of his father.

Realizing that his father was gone for the long forever, he was filled with remorse for his wild days, his disobediences, his unwillingness to do as his father had wished. The sensitive boy wept now with repentance and self-accusation.

His mother, trying to comfort him, said, "What's done is done and it can't matter to your father any longer. Now I want you to promise me...."

"I will promise you anything," the boy sobbed, "if you only won't make me go back to school. Anything."

A few days later Mark Twain was apprenticed to a printer with whom his family felt he would make a living and get an education. His pay for the two years of his apprenticeship was to be board and clothes.

Two years after he became a printer, Mark Twain was walking down the streets of Hannibal, Missouri, one afternoon when he picked up a piece of paper that was blowing along the sidewalk—a page that had been torn from a book.

That little incident, trivial as it was, probably affected Mark Twain's career more than any other single act of his life, for that stray bit of paper was a page torn from a biography of Joan of Arc. It told of her being held captive in the fortress at Rouen. The injustice of it all stirred this young boy of fourteen. Who was Joan of Arc? He didn't know. He had never even heard of her. But from then on, he devoured everything that had ever been written about her. His interest in her life story glowed and burned for more than half a lifetime; forty-six years later he wrote a book about her entitled *Recollections of Joan of Arc*. The critics felt that this book was far from his best, but he considered it his masterpiece. He knew that if it were published under his name, people would regard it as a humorous book; and he was so eager to have it taken seriously that he didn't even sign his name to it.

Albert Bigelow Paine says in his four-volume

biography of Mark Twain that finding the page about Joan of Arc awakened Mark Twain's interest in all history and fired him with a passion that became "the largest feature of his intellectual life and remained with him until his very last day on earth. From the moment when that fluttering leaf was blown into his hands, his career as one of the mentally elect was assured."

Mark Twain had no more business ability than a Kansas jack rabbit; he was a sucker for the most fantastic financial schemes. For example: as a result of reading a book, he once got the idea that he could make a fortune collecting and selling cocoa in the steaming jungles along the upper reaches of the Amazon River. He knew nothing about cocoa, had no money to pay for the long trip to South America, and even if he had reached the headwaters of the Amazon, he couldn't have talked to the natives and would probably have died of tropical fever. But incredible as it sounds, he found a fifty-dollar bill blowing down the street one day. He took that fifty dollars and started for the Amazon River. He got as far as Cincinnati and then had to give up the trip because he ran out of money.

Later in life he made vast profits from his books and lectures, but every time he tried to invest his money—well, let me give you some concrete examples. He invested in a patent steam generator that wouldn't generate. He invested in a watch company that didn't tick long enough to pay its first dividend. He invested in a steam pulley that wouldn't work. He started a publishing company that failed with a loss of 160,000 dollars. He invested heavily in a machine that was supposed to set type. The only thing it ever set was Mark Twain; it set him back about a fifth of a million dollars.

Then one day Mark Twain met a young inventor named Alexander Graham Bell. Bell tried to persuade Mark Twain to invest his money in a newfangled invention called the telephone. This man Bell actually claimed that with his invention you could sit in your own house and talk to somebody five blocks away—over a wire. Mark Twain laughed. He might be a fool, but he wasn't an idiot. The very idea of talking five blocks over a wire. Absurd!

If Mark Twain had bought five hundred dollars' worth of telephone stock then, it would be worth untold millions today. Instead of investing the five hundred dollars in telephone stock, however, Mark Twain loaned it to a friend who went bankrupt three days later.

In 1893, when Mark Twain was fifty-eight years old, he found himself overwhelmed with debts. The nation was trembling under the influence of a financial depression and Mark Twain himself was suffering from ill health. He could have by-passed his debts through bankruptcy. But he didn't. Instead, he resolved that he would pay back every cent he owed. How? By writing and by making a lecture tour of the world. Despite his ill health and his hatred of lecturing, he spent five years on a speaking tour, in order to pay his creditors. The tour was a tremendous success. It was almost impossible to find halls large enough to house the crowds that flocked to hear him. When the last dollar was paid, Mark Twain wrote: "I have abundant peace of mind again—no sense of burden. Work has become a pleasure—it is not labor any longer."

Mark Twain was infinitely more fortunate in love, however, than in business. Before he ever saw the girl he married, he fell in love with her picture. It happened while he was making a boat trip to the Holy Land—the trip that resulted in his writing *Innocents Abroad*.

One fateful day Mark Twain visited the cabin of

his young friend Charles Langdon and saw there a picture of Langdon's sister, the beautiful Olivia Langdon. In a flash he knew that that was the girl he wanted to marry. Again and again, as the boat trip progressed, he returned to young Langdon's cabin to look reverently at the miniature, and each time his conviction deepened that this was the girl for him.

A few months later Mark Twain met Olivia Langdon at a dinner in New York. Toward the end of his life, he wrote: "From the day I met her to now, she has never been out of my mind." Mark Twain was soon invited to visit at her father's house in Elmira, New York.

When the time came for the end of his visit, he did not want to leave. He got the Langdon's coachman to fix the carriage seat so it would upset and dump him out on the ground. Then he packed his bag, shook hands, climbed into the spring wagon and waved good-by. The coachman cracked his whip and the horses lunged forward. The back seat upset and quick as a flash there was Mark Twain on the ground with his eyes closed, apparently half dead. Well, of course, great excitement ensued. The family picked him up, carried him inside the house, and put him to bed. And for two mortal weeks he remained in bed. There wasn't a thing the matter with him—he'd learned that carriage trick when he was a boy in Hannibal, Missouri—but he lay there in bed and let himself be nursed and waited on and petted by his sweetheart. She called him "Youth, dear" and he called her "Livy, darling"; and until the time of her death, thirty-four years later, they were always "Livy, darling" and "Youth, dear." She kept his love letters locked up in a box; and every year when they went on their vacation, she sent them to the bank for safekeeping.

His wife edited all of Mark Twain's manuscripts. At night he took his day's writing and placed it on a stand by the head of her bed so she could read it before she went to sleep. She took out all the cuss words and saw that everything was perfectly proper. No matter what changes she made in his work, he always accepted them without argument.

He had such a horror of losing his manuscripts or misplacing them that he wouldn't let the maid dust his desk. He used to draw a chalk line on the floor, and the maid was forbidden to step across that line.

When Mark Twain reached seventy, he decided that he was old enough to do as he pleased; he ordered fourteen white suits and a hundred white ties, and for the rest of his life he wore nothing but white from head to foot. He even had a white dress suit.

Halley's comet was visible in the sky the night that Mark Twain was born in 1835. It returns every seventy-six years and it was his ambition to live until it appeared again. He did. Halley's comet was glowing in the sky again the night he died in 1910. His last request was that his daughter sing to him the old Scotch airs that he loved so well.

Here are four lines which Mark Twain had engraved on the tombstone of his daughter Susy—lines which a loving nation might well have engraved on his own headstone:

Warm summer sun, shine kindly here;
Warm Southern wind, blow softly here:
Green sod above, lie light, lie light!—
Good night, dear heart, good night, good night.

MARTIN JOHNSON

THREE LITTLE WORDS—"CAN YOU COOK?"
LED HIM TO THE ENDS OF THE EARTH

MARTIN JOHNSON, who photographed thousands of lions in the wilds of Africa, killed only two. He told me that during twenty months of his last stay in Africa, he saw more lions than he had ever seen before; yet he never fired a gun once. In fact, he didn't even carry a gun.

Some African explorers like to come back and tell about their blood-curdling experiences; but Martin Johnson believed that he or any other man who really knows the wild animals of Africa can walk from Cairo to the Cape armed with nothing more deadly than a bamboo walking stick and never suffer any harm.

He also told me that the last time he went to Africa, he took along a fine radio set so he could listen to programs from America. He said he listened a great deal for the first month or two, and then he got so tired of listening to long, blatant commercial announcements, that he didn't turn on the radio for months at a time.

Martin Johnson started roaming the world when he was fourteen years old. His father was a jeweler in Independence, Kansas, and when Martin was a boy, he used to unpack the crates that came from the far-flung corners of the compass. He was fascinated by the strange, colorful names on the labels—Paris, Geneva, Barcelona, Budapest—and he determined to put the dust of those towns under his heel. So one day he ran away, tramped over the United States, and finally shipped on a cattle boat to Europe. Landing in the Old World, he worked at anything he could find; but he couldn't always find work. He went hungry in Brussels; in Brest, he stood gazing out across the Atlantic, discouraged and homesick; and in London, he had to sleep in packing boxes. In order to get back to America and Kansas, he hid himself as a stowaway in the lifeboat of a steamship bound for New York.

Then something happened which changed the course of his whole existence, and set him out on trails of glamorous adventure. An engineer on the boat showed him a magazine containing an article by Jack London. Jack London told in this article how he intended to make a trip around the world in a little thirty-foot boat called the Snark.

As soon as Johnson arrived home in Independence, he wrote a letter to Jack London. He poured out his soul in eight feverish pages, and begged to go along on that trip. "I've already been abroad," he wrote. "I started from Chicago with $5.50 in my pocket, and when I got back, I still had twenty-five cents."

Two weeks passed — two weeks of nerve-wracking suspense. And then came a telegram from Jack London. It contained only three words — three words that changed Martin Johnson's life. "Can you cook?" the telegram inquired with telegraphic abruptness and brevity.

Could he cook? Why, he couldn't even cook rice. But he wired back precisely three words — "Just try me" — then he went out and got himself a job in the kitchen of a restaurant.

And when the *Snark* finally sailed across the rippling waters in San Francisco bay, and nosed her way out into the Pacific, Martin Johnson was aboard as chief cook and bottle washer, and his newly acquired culinary knowledge enabled him to make bread, omelets, gravy, soup, and even pudding. It was also his job to buy the provisions for the trip, and he calculated that he took along enough salt and pepper and other spices to last a normal crew something like two hundred years.

He learned to navigate during that trip. He thought he was an expert navigator. So one day, just to show how smart he was, he tried to locate the position of the ship on the map.

By that time, the *Snark* was in mid-Pacific swept along by billowing sails in the direction of Honolulu; but according to his nautical calculations, the ship was located squarely in the middle of the Atlantic Ocean!

But he didn't give a whoop if his calculations were all cock-eyed. He was living the gay, adventurous life every boy dreams of living. Nothing could daunt his enthusiasm. Once the crew ran out of water for two weeks and nearly perished under a sizzling sun—a sun so blasted hot that the pitch in the deck seams bubbled and boiled like soft molasses!

Many years have passed since then—years packed with action, for Martin Johnson sailed the seven seas and roamed all over the world from the coral islands of the South Seas to the jungles of darkest Africa. He made the first pictures of cannibals ever shown in this country.

He photographed pigmies and giants, elephants and giraffes, and made pictures of all the wild life on the African veldt. He brought back a whole Noah's Ark full of fantastic creatures—brought 'em back on spools of celluloid film that have been unreeled upon thousands of moving picture screens. He captured an imperishable record of a perishing wild animal life—a photographic record that your great grandchildren may enjoy generations from now when many of the wild animals of Africa no longer exist.

Martin Johnson told me that a well-fed lion that has never been molested by man will pay no attention whatever to the scent of a human being. He had driven his automobile into the midst of a bunch of fifteen lions, and the lions just lay there and blinked like pussy cats. One lion even came over and started to chew the front tire. Another time, he drove his car so close to a lioness that she could have reached out and touched it with her paw—but she didn't so much as twitch a whisker.

I asked him: "Are you trying to tell me that a lion is really *a good-natured* beast?"

And he said: "Good heavens, no! The best way I know to commit suicide is to trust a lion. Why, you never know when he's going to become suspicious and turn on you. And there's nothing in the world more dangerous than a charging lion. It's just like having a hundred pounds of dynamite coming at you. A lion can travel forty feet at a single leap, and he can cover ground faster than Cavalcade on the home stretch."

I asked him what he considered his narrowest escape, and he said: "Oh, there have been lots of close calls. But they're all fun."

One of his closest calls was in the South Sea Islands, when he nearly ended up in a kettle of soup. That was when he was getting the first pictures of cannibals ever made.

White traders had been raiding the cannibal islands, kidnaping the natives and selling them into slavery. The cannibals were hostile and suspicious— and hungry. They had already killed a number of white men and seized their goods; and after sizing up Martin Johnson, they figured that this chap from Kansas would make a nice tender pot roast for Sunday dinner.

So while he was busy talking to the chief and

laying out the presents he had brought along, dozens of cannibals began to gather out of the forest and surround him. Help was miles away. He had a revolver, but he was outnumbered a hundred to one. A cold sweat of fear stood out on his forehead. His heart raced and pounded; but there was nothing to do but to try to appear calm and keep on talking. And all the time he was being crowded in by a ring of greedy cannibals licking their chops in anticipation. For the first time since he'd left Independence, Kansas, Martin Johnson began to think it might not have been a bad idea after all if he'd gone into the jewelry business with his father.

And then, as the cannibals were about to rush, a miracle happened. Into the bay far below steamed a British patrol boat. The cannibals stared. They knew what that meant. Johnson stared too, hardly able to believe his own eyes. And then, with a low bow to the chief, he said: "You see, my ship has come after me. Glad to have met you all. Goodbye." And before anyone summoned enough courage to stop him, he made a dash for the shore.

HOWARD THURSTON

THE MISSIONARY WHO GOT ON THE
WRONG TRAIN—AND BECAME A
FAMOUS MAGICIAN

ONE COLD NIGHT, a crowd was pouring out of McVicker's Theatre in Chicago. It was a laughing, happy crowd—a crowd that had been entertained by Alexander Herrmann, the great magician of that day.

A shivering newsboy stood on the sidewalk, trying to sell copies of the *Chicago Tribune* to the crowd. But he was having a tough time of it. He had no overcoat, he had no home, and he had no money to pay for a bed. That night, after the crowd faded away, he wrapped himself in newspapers and slept on top of an iron grating which was warmed slightly by the furnace in the basement, in an alley back of the theatre.

As he lay there, hungry and shivering, he vowed that he too would be a magician. He longed to have crowds applauding him, wear a fur-lined coat, and have girls waiting for him at the stage door. So he made a solemn vow that when he was a famous magician, he would come back and play as a headliner in the same theatre.

That boy was Howard Thurston—and twenty years later he did precisely that. After his performance he went out in the alley and found his initials where he had carved them on the back of the theatre a quarter of a century before when he had been a hungry, homeless newsboy.

At the time of his death—April 13, 1936—Howard Thurston was the acknowledged dean of magicians, the king of legerdemain. During his last forty years he had traveled all over the world, time and again, creating illusions, mystifying audiences, and making people gasp with astonishment. More than sixty million people paid admissions to his show, and his profits were almost two million dollars.

Shortly before his death, I spent an evening with Thurston in the theatre, watching his act from the wings. Later we went up to his dressing room and he talked for hours about his exciting adventures. The plain, unvarnished truth about this magician's life was almost as astonishing as the illusions he created on the stage.

When he was a little boy, his father whipped him cruelly because he had driven a team of horses too fast. Blind with rage, he dashed out of the house, slammed the door, ran screaming down the street and disappeared. His mother and father never saw him or heard from him again for five years. They feared he was dead.

And he admitted that it was a wonder he wasn't killed; for he became a hobo, riding in box cars, begging, stealing, sleeping in barns and haystacks and deserted buildings. He was arrested dozens of times, chased, cursed, kicked, thrown off trains, and shot at.

He became a jockey and a gambler; at seventeen years of age, he found himself stranded in New York without a dollar, and without a friend. Then a significant thing happened. Drifting into a religious meeting, he heard an evangelist preach on the text, "There Is a Man in You."

Deeply moved, and stirred as he had never been stirred before in his life, he was convinced of his sins. So he walked up to the altar and with tears rolling down his checks, was converted. Two weeks later, this erstwhile hobo was out preaching on a street corner in Chinatown.

He was happier than he had ever been before, so he decided to become an evangelist, enrolled in the Moody Bible School at Northfield, Massachusetts, and worked as a janitor to pay for his board and room.

He was eighteen years old then, and up to that time, he had never gone to school more than six months in his life. He had learned to read by looking out of box car doors at signs along the railway and asking other tramps what they meant. He couldn't write or figure or spell. So he went to his classes in the Bible School and studied Greek and biology in the daytime, and studied reading and writing and arithmetic at night.

He finally decided to become a medical missionary and was on his way to attend the University of Pennsylvania when a little thing happened that changed the entire course of his life.

On his way from Massachusetts to Philadelphia, he had to change trains at Albany. While waiting for his train, he drifted into a theatre and watched Alexander Herrmann perform tricks of magic that kept the audience popeyed with wonder. Thurston had always been interested in magic. He had always tried to do card tricks. He longed to talk to his idol, his hero, Herrmann the Great Magician. He went to the hotel and got a room next to Herrmann's; he listened at the key-hole and walked up and down the corridor, trying to summon up enough courage to knock, but he couldn't.

The next morning he followed the famous magician to the railway station, and stood admiring him with silent awe. The magician was going to Syracuse. Thurston was going to New York—at least he thought he was. He intended to ask for a ticket to New York; but by mistake he too asked for a ticket to Syracuse.

That mistake altered his destiny. That mistake made him a magician instead of a medical missionary.

At the floodtide of his fame, Thurston got almost a thousand dollars a day for his show. But I often heard him say that the happiest days of his life were when he was getting a dollar a day for doing card tricks for a medicine show. His name was painted in blazing red letters across a streaming banner, and he was billed as "Thurston, the Magician of the North." He was from Columbus, Ohio, but that is North, if you are from Texas.

Thurston admitted that there were many people who knew as much about magic as he did. What, then, was the secret of his success?

His success was due to at least two things. First, he had the ability to put his personality across the foot-lights. He was a master showman, he knew human nature; and he said those qualities were just as important for a magician as a knowledge of magic. Everything he did, even the intonations of his voice and the lifting of an eyebrow, had been carefully rehearsed in advance, and his actions had been timed to split seconds.

And second, he loved his audience. Before the curtain went up, he stood in the wings, jumping up and down to shake himself wide awake.... and he kept saying: "I love my audience. I love to entertain them. I've got a grand job. I'm so happy. I'm so happy!"

He knew that if he wasn't happy, no one else would be.

WILLIAM RANDOLPH HEARST

TWO-CENT NEWSPAPERS BOUGHT HIM
CASTLES IN SPAIN, CUCKOO CLOCKS,
AND EGYPTIAN MUMMIES

HAVE YOU EVER wondered what you would do if you had a million dollars? William Randolph Hearst has an income of a million dollars a month—or thirty thousand dollars a day. During the time it will take you to peruse this short chapter, his income will mount by approximately one hundred dollars.

No one ever calls William Randolph Hearst, William. Even his most intimate friends call him "W. R.," and his seventy thousand employees always speak of him as "The Chief."

Millions of people read his many newspapers and magazines. He is the richest and most powerful publisher in the world. His name is a household word all over America; yet he himself is a man of mystery. The average person knows more about the private life of Mahatma Gandhi than he does about William Randolph Hearst.

The most astonishing thing I know about the most aggressive publisher in America is that he is reticent and shy. For half a century, he has been hobnobbing with celebrities; yet he actually dislikes being introduced to strangers.

He usually has anywhere from ten to sixty guests staying on his vast estate in California; but his favorite form of recreation is to steal away by himself and play solitaire. And when he is in New York, his favorite recreation is to go window shopping!

The most magnificent estate in the Western world is Hearst's ranch in California. It contains a quarter of a million acres of land and stretches for fifty miles along the rockbound coast of the ocean.

High on a wind-swept spot two thousand feet above the roar of the Pacific, he has erected a lordly group of Moorish Castles which he calls "The Enchanted Hill." He has lavished uncounted millions of dollars in furnishing these castles. The walls are adorned with Gobelin tapestries that once beautified the chateaux of France. The hushed halls are glorified by soft paintings from the brush of Rembrandt, Rubens and Raphael, canvasses that are immortal. His guests dine in a huge banquet hall surrounded by priceless objects of art; but at lunch, they are given paper napkins.

He has a collection of wild animals that would make Barnum's circus look like a side-show. Herds of zebras, buffaloes, giraffes and kangaroos roam over the hills; thousands of exotic birds dart among the trees, and lions and tigers roar and snarl in his private zoo.

A friend of mine, Frank Mason, used to buy antiques for Hearst in France. Hearst purchases entire shiploads of art treasures—even entire castles—and brings them to America in packing boxes with every stone and brick and piece of timber numbered and labeled to show where it belongs so he can erect the buildings here with exact fidelity.

He purchased so many objects of art that he finally had to buy a huge warehouse in New York to store the things he isn't using. This warehouse has twenty employees, it costs sixty thousand dollars a year to keep it going, and it contains everything from cuckoo clocks to Egyptian mummies.

William Randolph Hearst's father was a Missouri farmer. He headed west during the gold rush of

Forty-nine, walked two thousand miles across the plains beside a team of oxen and a covered wagon, fought Indians, discovered gold and made millions. As he grew older, he loved to sit in the shade of a big tree on his estate. A few years ago, his son, William Randolph Hearst, noticed that this tree was blocking the view of the ocean from one of his windows. He couldn't bear to think of destroying a tree his father had loved, so he paid $40,000 to have the tree moved thirty feet.

He is very fond of animals. For example, one day a group of motion picture executives flew up from Hollywood to hold a conference with Mr. Hearst, but he kept them waiting while he comforted a pet lizard that had lost a part of its tail. On another occasion, he sent his private yacht for a doctor at midnight and paid a medical fee of $500 because a pet guinea pig had broken its leg.

Hearst is an expert amateur photographer, and

takes thousands of pictures every year. He is also an expert shot with a rifle. One day while out on his yacht, he surprised his guests by holding his revolver at his hip, firing at a sea gull, and bringing it down on the wing.

He is an expert clog-dancer, an excellent mimic, and a good story-teller. His memory is almost like an encyclopedia. For example, if you asked him to name the wives of Henry the Eighth, or to call off the presidents of the United States, the chances are a hundred to one that he could do it without a hitch.

One day Jimmie Walker and Charlie Chaplin were visiting at Hearst's ranch, and they got into an argument over the exact phraseology of a certain quotation from the Bible; Hearst settled the argument by repeating the quotation word for word.

He loves to surround himself with young people; and he never permits anyone to mention death in his presence.

Hearst inherited thirty million dollars from his father. He could have led the life of an idler; but instead, he has worked from eight to fifteen hours a day for fifty years; and he vows he will never retire until God retires him.

LIONEL BARRYMORE

AT 26 HE WAS A STAR; AT 53 A HAS-BEEN;
AT 57 THE GREATEST ACTOR IN AMERICA

I WAS THERE that night in 1918 when Lionel Barrymore opened on Broadway as Milt Shanks in *The Copperhead*. It was a brilliant occasion, a triumph that made dramatic history. An excited audience leaped to its feet and cheered wildly and frantically through fifteen curtain calls.

Fifteen years later, I had a long talk with Lionel Barrymore in the Green Room at Metro-Goldwyn-Mayer's headquarters on Broadway. When he began talking about his struggles for recognition as an actor, I was astonished. "What? You? A Barrymore, with all the prestige and glamor of your family behind you—surely you never had to struggle!" I demanded.

He looked at me a moment and, in his low rumbling voice, replied: "Why, there ain't no such animal as you're talking about. A famous name is often a handicap."

The Barrymore kids had a strange and rather haphazard childhood. Their father, Maurice Barrymore, was one of the most charming and captivating men who ever made off-stage history with his escapades.

He would spend his last nickel to buy an animal. He used to ship bears home—bears and monkeys and wild cats and a wide assortment of dogs. John and Lionel spent one summer in a farm house on Staten Island with no one for company but an old

Negro servant and thirty-five dogs of all shapes, sizes and breeds.

When Lionel, Jack and Ethel Barrymore appeared in *Rasputin and the Empress,* Hollywood proudly announced that this was the first time they had all played together. But Hollywood was wrong. The three Barrymores made their debut together more than forty years ago. The theatre was a dilapidated barn in the rear of an actor's boarding house on Staten Island, and the audience was made up of kids from the neighborhood. Admission was a penny and the total box office receipts was thirty-seven cents. They played *Camille.* Ethel was the business manager and she paid Lionel and Jack ten cents each, and to their intense disgust, pocketed the remaining seventeen cents.

Neither Lionel nor John aspired to be stage stars. They both wanted to be artists, and Lionel studied art in Paris for a time.

I asked him if he was ever broke and hungry then, and he said, "Yes, lots of times, because I couldn't sell my sketches to the magazines. Of course, I could always get money by wiring home, but sometimes I didn't have enough money to send a wire. Jack and I had a studio down in Greenwich Village, too," he continued, "but we didn't have any money to buy furniture. In fact, we didn't even have a bed. So we slept on the floor; and when it got too cold, we covered ourselves with the books. There was another chap, a writer, living with us and he had a removable gold tooth; when we were broke, we pawned his tooth. I remember we tried every pawnshop on the East side, but we could never raise more than seventy cents on it."

At twenty-six, Lionel Barrymore was a star, with his name flashing in bright lights on Broadway. But at fifty-three, his fame was only a memory. While his handsome brother, John, was one of the highest-paid stars in the world, and his sister, Ethel, had a New York theatre named in her honor, Lionel was earning a quiet living out in Hollywood as a director.

His friends and family were shocked. They complained bitterly that the most talented dramatic actor in America was going to waste. But Lionel didn't complain.

He threw a skill and knowledge gained from thirty years behind the footlights, into directing pictures. He dreamed. He studied. He experimented. He was the first director ever to discover that the sound camera could be moved around the lot—a discovery that revolutionized talking pictures. He dazed the industry with such unforgettable films as Ruth Chatterton in *Madame X,* Lawrence Tibbett in *The Rogue Song* and Barbara Stanwyck in *Ten Cents a Dance*. He was fifty-three, and he honestly believed his acting days were over.

Just as he had resigned himself to directing for the rest of his career, he got his chance. Norma Shearer was making *A Free Soul*. A great actor was needed for the part of the father. Lionel Barrymore stepped in front of the camera and covered himself with glory. He won the medal of the Academy of Motion Picture Arts and Sciences. Then the very producers who had formerly regarded him as a "has-been" fought for his services. Hit followed upon hit—*The Yellow Ticket; Mata Hari; Grand Hotel; Rasputin and the Empress; Ah, Wilderness!*

I asked Lionel Barrymore if he was ever discouraged before he made his come-back in Hollywood. He replied, "No, I've been up and down all my life. Lots of people said I was through; but I never thought much about it. I was always too darn busy to worry about my troubles."

SOMERSET MAUGHAM

THE PLAY THAT "WASN'T WORTH BOTHERING ABOUT" BECAME THE GREATEST DRAMA SINCE HAMLET

WHAT WOULD YOU SAY is the greatest stage play ever written? When leading dramatic critics of New York voted, by secret ballot, on the ten greatest plays of all time, the first honors went to *Hamlet*. And they decided that the second greatest play ever written was not *Macbeth* nor *King Lear* nor *The Merchant of Venice*, but *Rain*. Yes, *Rain*, that tempestuous drama of sex and religion, fighting tooth and claw, in the South Seas—the play based on a short story by Somerset Maugham.

Maugham has made $200,000 out of Rain. Yet he didn't spend even five minutes writing the play.

This is how it happened: He wrote a short story called *Sadie Thompson*. He didn't think much of the story—but one night, John Colton was staying at his house, and Colton wanted something to read till he fell asleep. Maugham handed him the proofs of *Sadie Thompson*.

Colton was fascinated with the story. It thrilled him. He got out of bed and paced the floor, and in his imagination that night he saw it as a play—a drama that was destined to become immortal.

The next morning he rushed to Somerset Maugham. "There's a great play in that story." he told him, "I've been thinking about it all night. Put me to sleep, eh? I didn't sleep a wink!"

But Maugham wasn't impressed. "A play?" he said in his crisp British voice, "Oh yes, possibly—a morbid sort of play. Might run six weeks. But it isn't really worth bothering about. Not really." And the play that he didn't think worth bothering about made him a fifth of a million dollars.

When the play was finished, several producers turned it down. They were positive it would fail. Then Sam Harris accepted it. He wanted it for a young actress named Jeanne Eagels. But the agent for the play objected. He wanted someone who was better known.

Finally Jeanne Eagels got the part and played *Sadie Thompson* with a passion and power that made her the sensation of Broadway. She played to packed houses for four hundred and fifteen rip-roaring performances.

Somerset Maugham has written many distinguished books such as *Of Human Bondage*, *The Moon* and *Six-pence*, and *The Razor's Edge*, and he has written a score of successful dramas. But he didn't write his own most celebrated play.

Some people call him a genius now; but he was a financial failure for *eleven* years after he started writing. Think of it! This man who was destined to make a million dollars as an author earned only five hundred dollars a year for the first *eleven* years that he turned out stories and novels. Sometimes he went hungry.

He tried to get a job writing editorials on a salary basis; but he couldn't. "I had to keep on writing," Maugham told me, "because I just literally couldn't hold down a job."

His friends told him he was a fool to keep on trying to write. He had already been graduated from medical college, so they urged him to forget fiction and practice medicine. But nothing could swerve him from his determination to write his name large across the pages of English literature.

Bob Ripley of *Believe It Or Not* fame, once said to me: "A man will work and slave in obscurity for ten years and then become famous in ten minutes." That is about what happened to both Ripley and Maugham.

Here is how Somerset Maugham got his first break. Somebody's play had failed in London, and the manager of the theatre was looking around for something to replace it. He wasn't looking for a hit—just any old thing would do to fill in until he could get a real play into rehearsal. So he fished around in his desk, and pulled out a play by Somerset Maugham. *Lady Frederick*, it was called. He had had it in his desk for a year; he had read it; it wasn't much of a play—he knew that. But it might do for a few weeks. He put it on—and the miracle happened. *Lady Frederick* was a smash hit. It set all London talking. It tickled England as nothing had since the sparkling dialogue of Oscar Wilde.

Immediately every theatre manager in London begged for a play by Somerset Maugham. He dug old manuscripts out of his desk; and within a few weeks, *three* of his plays were playing to capacity houses.

Royalties came pouring in a golden flood. Publishers fell over each other bargaining for the work of this new genius. Society showered him with invitations; and after eleven years of oblivion, Somerset Maugham found himself the toast of Mayfair drawing rooms.

Maugham told me that he never writes after one o'clock. He says his brain goes dead in the afternoon. He always smokes his pipe and reads philosophy for an hour before he starts to write.

He told me that he isn't superstitious—nevertheless he has the sign of the Evil Eye stamped on the bindings of his books. He has the same curious design on the family plate. He has it on his stationery, and on his playing cards. He has it carved on the mantel above the fire-place, and he even has it carved above the entrance to his villa. But when I asked him if he really believed in it, he merely smiled.

CLARENCE DARROW

A SMALL-TOWN INSULT MADE HIM
THE GREATEST CRIMINAL LAWYER OF HIS TIME

A SCHOOL TEACHER boxed the ears of a little boy because he was restless and fidgety and squirming in his seat. She boxed his ears in front of the other pupils, and humiliated him so that he cried all the way home. He was only five years old at the time, but he felt that he had been treated with cruelty and injustice; he learned to hate cruelty and injustice with a hatred that kept him fighting all his life.

That boy's name was Clarence Darrow, probably

the best-known lawyer in America—and certainly the greatest *criminal* lawyer of his time. His name has flashed time and again in bold headlines across every newspaper in the land. He was a crusader, a rebel, a fighter, a champion of the underdog.

The first case he ever handled is still talked about by the old-timers in Ashtabula, Ohio. The burning issue involved was nothing more vital than the ownership of a second-hand set of harness worth five dollars. But to Clarence Darrow there was a principle at stake. Injustice had raised its snarling head and he fought it as he would have fought a Bengal tiger. He was paid only five dollars to fight the case; but he fought it, at his own expense, through seven courts for seven years—and won it.

Darrow said he had never been ambitious for money or prestige. He said he was always a lazy cuss. He started out in life teaching a country school. One day an incident happened which changed his whole career. There was a blacksmith in town who studied law when he wasn't busy shoeing horses. Clarence Darrow heard this blacksmith argue a law case in the tinsmith's shop. He was fascinated with the wit and eloquence of these country spellbinders. He loved a scrap himself; so he borrowed the blacksmith's law books and began to study law. On Monday morning, he would take his law books to school, and while his pupils were studying geography or arithmetic, he thumbed through the pages of his Blackstone.

He admitted he might have remained a country lawyer all his days if something hadn't happened to goad him into action.

He and his wife decided to buy a small house in Ashtabula, Ohio, from a dentist. The price was thirty-five hundred dollars. Darrow drew five hundred dollars out of the bank (and that, by the way, was all he had in the world) and agreed to pay the rest in yearly installments. The deal was almost finished when the dentist's wife refused point-blank to sign the papers.

"See here, young man," she said scornfully, "I don't believe you'll ever earn thirty-five hundred dollars in *all your life*."

Darrow was furious. He refused to live in such a town. So he shook the dust of Ashtabula off his feet and headed for Chicago.

His first year in Chicago he made only three hundred dollars—not even enough to pay his room rent. But the next year he made ten times that much—three thousand dollars—as a special attorney for the city.

"When my luck began to change," Darrow said, "everything seemed rapidly to come my way." Before long he was general attorney of the Chicago and North-western Railway Company, and well on his way to a big-money career. Then there was an explosion. A strike. Hatred! Riots! Bloodshed!

Darrow's sympathies were on the side of the strikers. When Eugene Debs, head of the railroad union was called to trial, Darrow threw up his job; and instead of defending the railroads, he defended the strikers. That was the first of Darrow's fiery, sensational trials—every one of them a milestone in courtroom history. Take, for example, the famous case of Leopold and Loeb, confessed murderers of little Bobby Franks. Public opinion was so shocked, so horrified, at the brutality of the crime that when Clarence Darrow undertook the defense of the two murderers, he was reviled and persecuted and called worse than a criminal for daring to defend the guilty boys. And why did he do it? "I went in," Darrow said, "to do what I could against the wave of hatred and malice. No client of mine has ever been put to death and if that should ever happen, I feel it would almost kill me. I have never been able to read the story of an execution. I always left town if possible on the day of a hanging. I am strongly against killing."

Society makes criminals, he said, and any man might be guilty of any crime.

Darrow himself knew what it is to face trial. He was once accused of bribing a jury, and had to use his powerful eloquence in his own defense. The most touching expression of gratitude he ever experienced was during his own trial. A former client of his met him and said, "Listen, you saved me from the gallows once when I was in trouble; and now you are in trouble and I'd like to help you out. I'll be glad to kill the chief witness against you, and it won't cost you a cent."

A few years ago, Darrow published a book, the story of his life; and I remember I stayed awake far into the night reading the chapter in which he outlined his philosophy of life.

"I am not sure of how much or how little I have really accomplished," he said. "I have blundered on my way and I have snatched as much enjoyment as possible from the stingy fates. Each day must be sufficient unto itself, keeping in view only the direction and the journey's end. I cannot realize that I am old. Where can the long day have gone? It has been only a short time since I started on the road with all the world before me and immeasurable time ahead for the journey I was to take: now the pilgrimage is almost over and the day is nearly done. How endless the unexplored road appeared to be and how short the foot-worn trail seems now."

CLYDE BEATTY

STICK HIS HEAD IN A LION'S MOUTH?
—NOT WITHOUT A GAS-MASK!

HE HAS BEEN CLAWED and chewed by tigers. He has felt a lion's teeth sink into his leg clear to the bone; elephants have mauled him; bears have trampled on him; he has been slashed by a black leopard and bitten by hyenas. He's been sent bleeding and torn to the hospital twenty-one times. And the last time, when Nero, the biggest of his lions, finished with him, he was in the hospital for ten weeks and nearly lost a leg.

Clyde Beatty has one of the most dangerous jobs

in the world. The life insurance companies realize that he may be ripped to pieces by savage claws at any time; so they refuse to gamble on his life. He is the only performer in the circus who can't get an insurance policy.

He told me he had sometimes thought of quitting the lion and tiger business; but he says that if he had to punch a time-clock in a factory, or some similar job it would kill him. And if he's got to die, he'd rather be *gored* to death than *bored* to death.

Clyde Beatty has spent half his thrilling and exciting lifetime—fifteen years of it—under the big top. As a kid back in Chillicothe, Ohio, he was crazy about the circus.

One exciting day the Barnum and Bailey circus came to town. A laundryman stuck up a poster in his window. A glamorous picture in yellow and purple and red, showing a heroic lion trainer bravely cracking his whip over a cageful of roaring, snarling cats from Africa. Beatty rushed inside and begged the owner of the laundry to give him the poster after the circus left town. The laundryman said, "Yes, I'll give it to you if you'll run errands for me for a week." He agreed to this.

This twelve-year-old kid already had some roaring, snapping, snarling fiends of his own. Or at least, he made believe they were. He had five dogs which he had trained to sit up and beg, roll over, and walk around on their hind legs.

And every so often he would stick up his circus poster and put on a wild animal act for the kids in the neighborhood. Every year after that, when the circus came to town, he went and begged for a job. But he was too young.

Then one summer when the big caravan chugged out of town, Clyde Beatty was aboard, his heart palpitating with excitement. For three days, his desperate parents searched for him frantically. His mother spent nights of weeping before a letter came saying he had a job cleaning out the cages with the circus. He was only fifteen and he was getting five dollars a month and a chance to live in Paradise.

In ten years' time, this youngster from Chillicothe, Ohio had outstripped every lion-trainer in history. He put on an act so daring, so fool-hardy, that even circus men themselves said it couldn't be done.

And when they saw him actually do it, they said he was a lunatic and that his life wasn't worth a plugged nickel. He put forty snarling, spitting lions and tigers into the same cage, whacked his whip, and made them do their stuff. Forty lions and tigers bristling with hate and snarling with rage. No wonder the act created a sensation even among circus people, for lions and tigers are mortal enemies—they fight on sight. And on more than one occasion, Beatty has found himself in a cage full of fighting, roaring, murderous jungle cats.

Yet strangely enough, Clyde Beatty says that lions and tigers are *not* the most dangerous animals to control. He's tried them all—lions and tigers, leopards, bears, hyenas, and elephants. And he has found that the most dangerous beast of all is the polar bear.

And he says the hardest trick of all is to make a tiger ride on an elephant's back. In fact, he himself was nearly killed by an elephant one day, just because he had been to the tiger cage, and the elephant caught the hated scent of the tiger.

You've heard, haven't you, that animal trainers control their animals by looking them straight in the eye? Clyde Beatty told me that that is a lot of nonsense. The average lion wouldn't give two hoots even if Mae West looked him in the eye. He says the only reason he watches his animal's eyes is to find out what they're up to and what they're going to do next.

Beatty says no trainer has ever actually stuck his head in a lion's mouth. It just looks that way. He says: "I've known some pretty reckless animal trainers, but I have never heard of one crazy enough to stick his head inside the mouth of a lion." Besides, lions have halitosis so bad that even their best friends would have to wear gas-masks.

There's another popular idea—that lion-trainers use red-hot pokers to control enraged animals. But Beatty says that if you want to commit suicide, just enter the cage of a lion or a tiger that has been burned with a red-hot poker. His harmless weapons are a kitchen chair, a whip, and a revolver filled with blank cartridges.

And if there's one thing that gets his goat, it's to be called a *lion-tamer*. He's not a lion-tamer, he's a *lion-trainer*.

He says his lions are not tame—and neither are

his tigers. In fact, they're just about as wild as they were when they snarled in the jungles of Asia or Africa.

Clyde Beatty says he's tried working with tame animals—animals born in captivity, and he prefers wild ones any time.

Tame animals are just like spoiled children—they've been pampered and petted until they refuse to do anything.

The question he has been asked most often is this: can a lion lick a tiger, or will the tiger lick the lion? Frankly, he doesn't know. He's been in the big cage dozens of times with lions and tigers fighting all around him, but the lions always gang up and the tiger fights alone. When one lion starts fighting, all the lions in sight come to his aid—especially if the lions are brothers. Lions are just like boys—they can't see a scrap without mixing up in it. But a tiger has no race consciousness—he will sit up on his pedestal and actually yawn while some other tiger is being killed.

One of the most amusing stunts Clyde Beatty does in the Big Cage is to make a bear turn a complete somersault—the only trick of its kind in the world. He discovered it by accident. Beatty was in the cage one day when the bear came tearing at him, teeth bared, claws tense, and murder in his eye. This bear was out to kill, and his onslaught was so sudden, so fierce, that Beatty did the first thing that flashed to his mind.

He hauled off and smashed the bear on the nose. Nothing else is so painful to a bear as a poke on the nose; and as Beatty's fist landed, the bear went over in a heap and turned a complete somersault. That's what gave Beatty the idea.

And today all he has to do to make that same bear turn a complete flip-flop, is to tap him gently on the nose with his whip.

Clyde Beatty knows the wild animals of the jungle and plain—knows them better than any other man living. Yet he says his favorite animal is the dog.

THE MAYO BROTHERS

THE ILL-WIND THAT WRECKED A WHOLE TOWN—AND MAY YET SAVE THE WORLD FROM INSANITY

ONE OF THE MOST startling discoveries in the history of medicine might never have been made if a tornado hadn't wrecked a town in Minnesota a little over a half a century ago.

The town the tornado struck was Rochester, now world-famous as the home of the Mayo Brothers, two of the greatest surgeons in the history of medicine. And the discovery is a drug to cure insanity. This drug is injected into the body of a feeble-minded or insane person, and presto! the circulation of the blood is changed and the person is restored to sanity.

What could this discovery mean to humanity? Well, here are some facts. Figure it out for yourself.

There are more patients suffering from mental diseases in the hospitals in the United States than from all other diseases combined. One student out of every sixteen in our high schools today will spend part of his life in an insane asylum. If you are fifteen years of age and residing in New York State, the chances are one out of twenty that you will be confined in an institution for the mentally ill for seven years of your life. During the last decade, mental diseases have almost doubled in the United States. If this appalling rate of increase continues for another century, half the entire population of the United States will be in the insane asylums and the other half will be outside trying to support them by taxes.

The Mayo Brothers, who worked on this amazing remedy, were among the most celebrated surgeons in the world. Physicians from Paris, London, Berlin, Rome, Leningrad and Tokyo journeyed to Rochester Minnesota, to sit at their feet and learn. Sixty thousand patients a year, most of them facing their last chance against death, make pilgrimages to the Mayo clinic as to a Holy Shrine.

Yet, to repeat — if a tornado hadn't twisted and roared through the middle west over sixty years ago, the work would probably never have heard of the Mayo Brothers or Rochester, Minnesota, or this cure for insanity.

When Doctor Mayo — the father of the Mayo Brothers — settled there eighty years ago, Rochester had only two thousand people. His first two patients were a sick cow and a sick horse.

When the Indian wars broke out, Doctor Mayo grabbed his musket and made the redskins bite the dust. When the smoke of battle cleared away, he picked his way over the battle ground laying out the dead and treating the wounded. His regular patients were scattered for fifty miles over the prairies of Minnesota. Many of them lived in houses made of prairie sod. They couldn't afford to pay a physician, but good old Doctor Mayo sometimes traveled all night to allay their aches and pains. Sometimes he fought his way through snow storms and blizzards so blinding that he couldn't see his hand before him in broad daylight.

He had two sons, William and Charles, later famous throughout the world as the Mayo Brothers.

They worked in a local drugstore, learned how to fill prescriptions and pound up pills, went to medical college—and then a tragedy occurred, a tragedy destined to affect the history of medicine.

The tragedy was this: a cyclone, a tornado, swept over the prairies of Minnesota like an angry god. It blasted, it demolished, it smashed to smithereens everything in the path of its fury. It struck Rochester and knocked it into a cocked hat. Hundreds of people were wounded and twenty-three were killed. For days, the Mayo Brothers and their father worked among the ruins, bandaging wounds, setting broken limbs, and performing operations. Sister Alfred, Mother Superior of the Convent Sisters of St. Francis, was so impressed with their work that she offered to build a hospital if the Mayos would take charge of it. They agreed, and when the Mayo clinic was opened in 1889, old Doctor Mayo was a man of seventy and his two sons had never even served as hospital internes. "We were the greenest of a green crew"—that is the way they described themselves. Yet William Mayo, the older brother, became the world's greatest authority on cancer. Each brother believed the other the greater man—and both were famous for the cleanest work that surgery has every known. They worked surely and swiftly—with a swiftness that astonished most surgeons. Arriving at the clinic at seven in the morning, they operated constantly for four hours every day. They performed from fifteen to thirty operations a day for years. And yet they both continued to study, tried to improve their work—and they admitted that they had much to learn. The entire city of Rochester now exists by and for the Mayo clinic. No street cars are allowed. The buses run silently and even the conversation in the streets is hushed.

Paupers and bank presidents, farmers and movie stars all have to take their turns in the waiting room, and all are treated alike. The rich pay according to their means, but no one has ever been turned away because he was unable to pay.

One third of the Mayo Brothers' work was charity. They never sued for bills, they never took notes, and they never permitted a man to mortgage his home in order to pay them. They took in cash whatever a man could afford to pay at the time and let it go at that, and they never asked a man how much he could afford to pay before they performed the operation.

One man mortgaged his farm to pay them for saving his life; and when they discovered what he had done, they returned his check and sent him a check of their own for several hundred dollars to compensate him for the loss he had sustained in his illness.

They are glorious examples of two small town boys who were never interested in making money; and yet it poured in upon them in a golden flood.

They didn't care for fame; yet they became the most famous surgeons in the United States.

Their sole desire was to aid suffering humanity. Over the desk in their waiting room hung a framed inscription which explains the eternal truth of their success. That sign read: "Have something the world wants and though you dwell in the midst of a forest, it will wear a beaten pathway to your door."

LEO TOLSTOY

HE WAS ASHAMED OF HAVING WRITTEN
TWO OF THE WORLD'S GREATEST NOVELS

◠ HERE IS A LIFE-STORY as incredible as any tale out of the Arabian Nights. It's the story of a prophet who died in our own time—in 1910, to be exact—and who was so venerated that for twenty years before he died an unbroken and unending stream of admirers made pilgrimage to his home in order to catch a glimpse of his face, hear the sound of his voice, or touch the hem of his garment.

Friends came and lived in his home for years at a

time and took down in shorthand every word that he uttered, even in the most casual conversation, and described in minutest detail even the most trivial acts of his daily life. These records were then printed in huge volumes.

Nearly 23,000 books—not 2300, mind you, but 23,000 books—and 56,000 newspaper and magazine articles have been written about this man and his ideas; and his own writings fill 100 volumes—a gigantic amount of words for any man to have written.

The story of his life is as colorful as some of his own novels. He was born in a forty-two room mansion, surrounded by wealth, cradled in the luxury of the old Russian aristocracy; yet in the last part of his life he gave away all of his lands, stripped himself of all his worldly goods, and died without a dollar in a lonely Russian railway station, surrounded by peasants.

In his youth, he was a snob, walking with mincing steps and spending a small fortune in the tailor shops of Moscow; yet in his later life he dressed in the rough crude clothes of a Russian peasant, made his shoes with his own hands, tended his own bed, swept his own room and ate his simple food on a bare table from a wooden bowl with a wooden spoon.

In his youth he lived what he himself described as "a dirty, vicious life," drinking, duelling, committing every sin imaginable —even murder; but in later years he tried to follow literally the teachings of Jesus and became the most saintly influence in all of Holy Russia.

In the early years of his married life he and his wife were so happy that they actually got down on their knees and prayed to Almighty God to continue their heavenly bliss, their divine ecstasy. Yet later on they were tragically unhappy. He finally came to loathe the very sight of her, and his dying request was that his wife should not even be permitted to come into his presence.

In his youth, he failed in college and his private teachers despaired of ever pounding any sense whatever into his thick skull; yet thirty years later he wrote two of the greatest novels that the world has ever known, two novels that will live and endure throughout the centuries—*War and Peace*, and *Anna Karenina*.

Tolstoy is more famous today outside of Russia than all the Czars who ever ruled that dark and bloody empire. Yet did the writing of these great novels make him happy? For a while—yes. Then he became utterly ashamed of them, and devoted the remainder of his life to writing little pamphlets, preaching peace and love and the abolition of poverty. These booklets were printed in cheap editions and trundled about in carts and wheelbarrows and sold from door to door. In four short years 12,000,000 copies were distributed.

A few years ago it was my privilege to know Tolstoy's youngest daughter in Paris. She acted as his secretary during the last years of his life and she was with him when he died. I learned from her own lips many of these facts about Tolstoy. Since that time, she has written a book about her father, *The Tragedy of Tolstoy*.

Truly Tolstoy's life was a tragedy, and the cause of his tragedy was his marriage. His wife loved luxury, but he despised it. She craved fame and the plaudits of society, but these frivolous things meant nothing whatever to him. She longed for money and riches, but he believed that wealth and private property were a sin. She believed in ruling by force, but he believed in ruling by love.

And to make matters worse, she was consumed by a fierce and fiery jealousy. She detested his friends.

She even drove her own daughter away from her home, and then rushed into Tolstoy's room and shot at the girl's picture with an air rifle.

For years she nagged and scolded and screamed and abused him and, as he said, turned his home into a veritable hell because he insisted on giving the people of Russia the right to publish his books freely without paying him royalty.

When he opposed her, she threw herself into fits of hysteria, rolling on the floor with a bottle of opium to her lips, swearing that she was going to kill herself and threatening to jump down the well.

The Tolstoys were married almost half a century; and sometimes she knelt at his knees and implored him to read to her the exquisite, poignant love passages that he had written about her in his diary forty-eight years previously, when they were both madly in love with each other. As he read of those beautiful happy days that were now gone forever, both of them wept bitterly.

Finally, when he was eighty-two years old, he was unable to endure the tragic unhappiness of his home any longer, so he fled from his wife on the night of October 21, 1910—fled into the cold and darkness, not knowing whither he was going.

Eleven days later he died of pneumonia in a railway station-house, saying, "God will arrange everything." His last words were, "To seek—always to seek."

21

J. PIERPONT MORGAN

THEY CAME AFTER HIM WITH GUNS
AND T.N.T.—BUT HE STILL RAISED EASTER LILIES

PROBABLY THE MOST powerful man in the world of *finance* was J. Pierpont Morgan, Dictator of Wall Street, High Mogul of the World of Stocks and Bonds.

Yet, as a person, he was almost totally unknown. It would hardly be an exaggeration to call him a man of mystery. He shunned publicity, and his hatred of photographers amounted to a phobia.

When angered, he was blunt to the point of indiscretion. In fact, he was so outspoken he was sometimes called "the most undiplomatic man in America."

Six feet tall, with two hundred pounds of dauntless physical courage, he was utterly without fear. For example, one day a maniac forced his way into Morgan's house, whipped out a gun, and threatened to shoot. Morgan might have dodged through a nearby door, but he didn't. Instead, he walked straight toward the gleaming pistol. Instantly there was a crack of an explosion. Morgan staggered. The bullet had plowed into his abdomen. He staggered, but he kept on coming, He leaped upon the madman, wrenched the pistol from his hand. Then Morgan collapsed and fell to the floor unconscious. He was rushed away to a hospital. Death had missed him by a fraction of an inch.

It was almost impossible for an ordinary mortal to approach the mighty King of Gold in his office at 23 Wall Street—that low, squat citadel of high finance which is known simply as "The Corner." The sight-seeing guides never fail to point out to tourists the scars on the face of that building—sole reminder today of that hideous disaster of 1916 that wiped out the lives of forty people, injured two hundred more, and destroyed two million dollars' worth of property.

It happened precisely at one minute past noon. Happy, carefree crowds were pouring out of a thousand office and no one paid any attention to a decrepit old horse and wagon that stood opposite the Morgan citadel.

Suddenly there was a blinding sheet of saffron-green light. Then a blast—a terrific explosion—that rocked the mighty skyscrapers on their very foundations. A bomb had burst,—a bomb loaded with a hundred pounds of T.N.T. A hail of deadly shrapnel swept the street.

A thousand windows were splintered to bits, a

storm of broken glass roared down to the pavement. Awnings twelve stories above the earth suddenly burst into flame.

Arms, legs, and even human heads were hurled through windows twenty and thirty feet above the side-walk, and flung upon ledges.

Men maimed, bleeding, and dying ran shrieking through the streets, only to fall headlong in death.

The sirens of fire engines and the screaming of ambulances added to the bedlam of panic and fear.

And when the chaos was cleared away, all that remained of the horse and wagon that had brought the bomb was a bit of a wheel, two horseshoes, and a few nuts and bolts.

But Morgan, at whom all this was aimed, was in Europe at the time. He determined to capture the criminals responsible for that dastardly deed—to capture them no matter what the cost.

A reward of fifty thousand dollars was offered.

The New York police, Federal agents, Secret Service men, private detectives, started one of the biggest man-hunts in history. The search led all over the earth. Departing ships were watched—and so were the Canadian and Mexican borders. The underworld of New York and Chicago and a dozen other cities were combed for clues. A king's ransom was spent in the search; but it ended in futility.

Two armed detectives kept constant vigil in front of the Morgan offices; and the roof of his low building was covered with heavy iron screening to protect it from bombs which might be hurled from neighboring skyscrapers.

In the inner sanctum of that solid, unostentatious building stretched two rows of desks, one behind the other, like seats in a school-room. At these desks worked the eighteen Morgan partners—and at the very back of them all, like a schoolmaster supervising a class at examination time, sat Morgan, the head of the firm.

No other private banking house in the history of the world has played so important a role in the feverish affairs of nations. Not even the Medicis of Florence or the Rothschilds of Europe have enjoyed such far-flung prestige. The Rothschilds saved Europe from Napoleon; but Morgan, more than any other single financial force, made the Allies victorious in the first World War.

In 1915, Morgan & Co. floated the hugest foreign loan ever dreamed of. Five hundred million dollars—half a billion—went across the seas to serve as the sinews of war. The Morgans became the purchasing agents in the United States for the whole Allied armies. They bought billions upon billions of dollars' worth of arms and supplies. In one month, they spent more money than ordinarily passes hands over the entire surface of the globe in a like amount of time.

J. P. Morgan was as much at home in the pea-soup fog of London as he was in the roar and soot of New York. For years, while his father was living, he was head of the English branch of Morgan & Co., and when he came back to Wall Street, he introduced the English custom of having tea in the afternoon.

He had a house in Grosvenor Square, London, equipped with a full staff of servants, so that he could drop in any time—even after months of absence—and find the table ready for dinner, a fire roaring up the chimney, and the covers of his bed turned down.

He was the greatest pillar of the Episcopal Church in America, yet he corresponded regularly with Pope Pius XI in Rome. And when he visited the Vatican, he and the Pope sat for hours discussing—what do you, suppose?—rare manuscripts written in Coptic, the medieval language of Egypt.

Mr. Morgan's private library houses many

illuminated manuscripts written by the old monks five hundred years before Columbus discovered America. He possessed priceless folios of Shakespeare and a copy of the Gutenberg Bible. That one book alone is probably worth a fifth of a million dollars.

J. P. Morgan was famous for his knowledge of Shakespeare and the Bible; yet he dearly loved to settle down to a good detective story, even as you and I.

Like his father, who was known as Morgan the Magnificent, he was a great connoisseur of art. He spent uncounted millions on paintings, sculpture, tapestries, porcelains, and jewelry. And when he sold some of his priceless paintings, the story was flung in headlines across the front pages of every paper in New York.

On each Christmas Eve, a unique ceremony took place in the Morgan Library. The children and grand-children, and a few intimate friends gathered round and listened to the story of Scrooge as told in A Christmas Carol. The story was read not from a printed book, but from the original manuscript written in Dickens' own handwriting.

In spite of all his wealth, many of Morgan's pleasures were very simple. For example, he loved to put on an old hat and coat and walk while the rain beat and lashed his face.

He adored his wife, and after her death in 1925, he kept her room exactly as she left it. She succumbed to that mysterious disease known as sleeping sickness, and all of Morgan's millions were powerless to save the woman he loved.

EVANGELINE BOOTH

THE SPINSTER WHO TURNED DOWN THE MARRIAGE PROPOSALS OF A THOUSAND MEN AND RODE A SNORTING, BUCKING HORSE

THE MOST WONDERFUL WOMAN I have ever known had a thousand men propose to her. She has turned down offers from millionaires and from fisher-men and farmers and penniless men on the Bowery. A prince from one of Europe's most prominent royal families followed her for months and begged her to marry him. And after she had already reached her three-score years and ten, she was still getting so many proposals by mail that her secretary didn't even bother to show them to her.

Her name is Evangeline Booth, and until her retirement in 1939 she was the head of the grandest army that ever attacked an enemy—the Salvation Army—an army with thirty thousand officers, feeding the hungry in eighty-six far-flung countries and spreading love in eighty different languages.

I got something of a shock when I met Evangeline Booth. I knew she was old enough to be a grandmother, yet her dark red hair was just beginning to show a few streaks of gray. And she was sparkling with vivacity and blazing with enthusiasm.

Talk about life beginning at forty! If you ever saw this woman mount a horse that is so wild and jumpy that it takes two men to hold him, you would believe that life begins at seventy. Evangeline Booth bought the horse cheap because his owner was afraid to ride him. His name was Golden Heart, and when she mounted Golden Heart and shouted, "Let him go!"

Golden Heart jumped and plunged and went backwards and forwards and sideways all over the lot before she could quiet him down. She rode for an hour every morning—sometimes she held the reins in one hand and a speech in the other and prepared a talk while she was galloping through the woods.

Every summer when she was in America, she went to Lake George and did fancy diving—jack-knives and turtle-backs and swan-dives; and when she was sixty-three, she swam clear across Lake George in four hours.

She slept every night with a paper pad beside her bed, and often she awoke in the middle of the night and wrote down a sheaf of notes. One night when she couldn't sleep, she got up at 3:00 A.M. and composed the words and music to a song.

Evangeline Booth said that one of the most thrilling experiences of her life occurred during the gold rush to the Yukon. You may recall that just before the turn of the century, gold was discovered in Alaska, and the news set the nation seething with excitement. Hordes of men began hurrying to the far North, and Evangeline Booth knew that the Salvation Army would be needed there; so with a couple of trained nurses and three or four assistants, she headed for the Yukon. When she landed in Skagway, eggs were worth twenty-five cents apiece, and butter sold for three dollars a pound. Some men were hungry and all of them carried guns. And everywhere she heard men talking about "Soapy" Smith, the killer of the Klondike, the Dillinger of the Yukon. "Soapy" Smith and his gang laid in wait for miners returning from the gold fields and shot them down without warning and robbed them of their gold dust. The United States Government sent an armed posse to kill him; but "Soapy" Smith shot all of them and escaped.

Skagway was a tough place. Five men were killed

there the day Evangeline Booth arrived.

That night, she held a meeting on the banks of the Yukon River; and preached to twenty-five thousand lonely men and got all of them singing songs they had heard their mothers sing in the long ago—*Jesus, Lover of My Soul, Nearer My God To Thee*, and *Home, Sweet Home*.

The Arctic night was chilly and raw and cold, so while she was singing, one man brought a blanket and threw it around her.

This vast crowd of men sang until one o'clock in the morning; and then Evangeline Booth and her helpers went out in the forest to sleep on the ground under the pine trees. They had started a fire and were making a little cocoa when they saw five men approaching them with guns. When they got within speaking distance, the head man took off his hat and said, "I'm 'Soapy' Smith; and I've come to tell you how much I enjoyed your singing." And he added,

"I was the man that sent you the blanket while you were singing. You can keep it, if you want to." A blanket doesn't sound like much of a gift now; but it was a royal present up there where men were dying from chills and the damp.

She asked him if she would be in any danger there in Skagway. "No. Not while I'm here," he said. "I'll protect you."

She talked with him in the white night of the midnight sun for three hours. She said, "I'm giving life and you're taking it. That's not right. You can't win. They'll kill you sooner or later." She talked to him of his childhood and his mother; and he told her that he used to attend Salvation Army meetings with his grandmother and sing and clap his hands. And he confessed that when his grandmother lay dying, she asked him to sing a song they had learned together at the Salvation Army meetings:

My heart is now whiter than snow,
For Jesus abides with me here.
My sins which are many, I know
Are pardoned. My title is clear.

Miss Booth asked him to kneel with her; and the Salvation Army girl and "Soapy" Smith, the most notorious bandit that ever terrorized the North, got down on their knees together and prayed and wept together under the northern pines. With tears rolling down his cheeks, "Soapy" promised her that he would stop killing people and would give himself up, and Miss Booth promised that she would use all her influence with the government to get him a light sentence.

At four o'clock in the morning, he left her.

At nine o'clock, he sent one of his men to her with a present of freshly baked bread and jam tartlets and a find of butter—delicacies that were priceless up there. He had stuck people up with a gun and stolen the flour and the butter, and one of the bad women of Skagway had requested the privilege of baking the bread and jam tartlets for the good woman who had come to Alaska to preach love and purity and forgiveness.

Two days later, somebody shot "Soapy" Smith and Skagway erected a monument to the honor of the man who killed him.

Evangeline Booth was one of the happiest persons I have ever met. Happy because she was living for others. She told me that the deepest passion of her life was a desire to make every person she met—even every waitress and Pullman porter—a little better because she had passed that way.

BILLY SUNDAY

THE BALLPLAYER WHO LED A MILLION
SOULS DOWN THE SAWDUST TRAIL TO SALVATION

⁓ THE MOST POPULAR PREACHER in the history of the Christian pulpit was an ex-boozefighter and ex-ballplayer—Billy Sunday. Eighty million people—two thirds of all the men, women and children in America—flocked to hear his rough-and-ready, rip-snorting message of sin and salvation.

It was his favorite boast that during his thirty-five years of lambasting the devil, he had led more than a million souls down the sawdust trail toward the

Light, and he was probably the greatest single power in bringing about Prohibition.

I saw Billy Sunday many times. He was a fury, a human dynamo in trousers. I saw him thump his chest, tear off his coat, collar and tie, leap up on chairs, stand with one foot on the pulpit, and then fling himself on the floor in imitation of a ballplayer sliding in to home plate. Nobody ever went to sleep listening to Billy Sunday. His sermons were as entertaining as a circus. He preached so strenuously that he carried a physical trainer with him and never a day passed that he didn't get a pummelling and a rub-down.

He preached in Pittsburgh for eight weeks and the newspapers reported his meetings with flaring headlines every day. The whole town was excited. Big department stores sent their employees en masse to hear him. Factory girls attended the noon-day meetings in crowds. One day, ten policemen stepped forward before an audience of fifteen thousand people and declared themselves on the side of the Lord.

Unlike most evangelists, Billy Sunday appealed, mostly to men. He used to say: "I am a rube of the rubes. The odor of the barnyard is on me yet. I have greased my hair with goose grease and blacked my boots with stove blacking. I have wiped my old proboscis with a gunny-sack towel, I have drunk coffee out of my saucer, and I have eaten with my knife. I have said 'done it' when I should have said 'did it,' and I have said 'I have saw' when I should have said 'I have seen,' and I expect to go to heaven just the same."

He was born in a log cabin in Iowa and reared in an orphan asylum. When he was fifteen, he got a job as janitor in a school. This job paid him $25 a month and gave him a chance to get an education. All he had to do was to get up at two o'clock in the morning, carry coal for fourteen stoves, keep all fourteen fires going during the day, sweep and polish the floors, and then keep abreast in his studies.

His first real job was as assistant to an undertaker in Marshalltown, Iowa. It was while holding down that job that he began to make a name for himself as a ballplayer.

He could run the bases so fast that Pop Anson, leader of the Chicago White Sox, sent for him; and before Billy Sunday was twenty-one, he was a star performer in the big leagues. "I could circle those bases in fourteen seconds," he used to say, "and that's a record that's never been beaten."

It was five years after he left the undertaker's shop that the revelation occurred which changed him from a hard-drinking ballplayer into the most hypnotic preacher since the days of John Wesley.

Here is what happened to him—and now I am

quoting Billy Sunday's own words:

"One day in 1887, I was walking down a street in Chicago in company with some famous ballplayers. We went into a saloon. It was Sunday afternoon and we got tanked up and then went and sat down on a corner. Across the street a company of men and women were playing on instruments—horns, flutes and slide trombones—and the others were singing the gospel hymns that I used to hear my mother sing back in the log cabin in Iowa, and I sobbed and sobbed. Then a young man stepped out and said, 'We are going down to the Pacific Garden Mission. Won't you come down to the Mission with us? I am sure you will enjoy it. You will hear drunkards tell how they have been saved and girls tell how they have been saved from the red-light district.'

I arose and said to the boys, 'I'm through. I am going to Jesus Christ. We've come to the parting of the ways,' and I turned my back on them. Some of them laughed and some of them mocked me; but one of them gave me encouragement."

That is the way he described his own conversion.

The skeptics and scoffers used to accuse Billy Sunday of exploiting religious hunger for the mere sake of money. Yet the truth is, he gave up a salary of five hundred dollars a month as a ballplayer to work for the Y.M.C.A. for eighty-three dollars a month—and it was sometimes six months before he collected even that!

I remember Billy Sunday when he came to New York in 1917. Never before or since has the town called Babylon-on-the-Hudson seen such a frenzy of religious excitement. His arrival was heralded months in advance. At least twenty thousand prayer meetings were held in preparation for his coming. Up at 168th Street and Broadway, four hundred workers labored furiously to complete a tabernacle capable of seating twenty thousand, and four carloads of sawdust were sprinkled on the floor to make the famous sawdust trail. Two thousand chairs were placed upon the platform for the choir alone; and two thousand ushers, working in shifts of seven hundred each, volunteered for the honor of showing the faithful to their seats.

During his stay in New York, Billy Sunday preached to a million and a quarter people; and nearly a hundred thousand sinners came forward and renounced their evil ways.

THEODORE ROOSEVELT

HE WAS SHOT IN THE BREAST;
BUT HE KEPT RIGHT ON WITH HIS SPEECH

AN INCIDENT happened in January 1919 that I shall never forget. I was in the army at the time—stationed at Camp Upton on Long Island. One afternoon a detachment of soldiers marched up a hill, raised their rifles into the air, and fired a salute. Roosevelt was dead! Theodore Roosevelt, the most colorful and spectacular president that ever wielded a big stick over this nation! He died a comparatively young man.

Almost everything about Teddy Roosevelt was extraordinary. For example, even though he was so near-sighted that, without his glasses, he couldn't recognize his best friend ten feet away, he became an expert rifle shot and brought down charging lions in Africa.

He was the most famous big-game hunter of all time; yet he never went fishing, and never shot a bird.

As a boy, he was pale and sickly and tortured with asthma; so he went west for his health, became a cowboy, slept out under the stars, and developed such a magnificent physique that he boxed with Mike Donovan. He explored the wilderness of South America, climbed such mountains as the Jungfrau and the Matterhorn, and led a mighty charge up San Juan Hill in Cuba in the face of deadly rifle fire.

Roosevelt says in his autobiography that as a child he was nervous and timid and afraid of getting hurt;

yet he broke his wrist, his arm, his nose, his ribs, and his shoulder, and kept right on taking chances. When he was a cowboy in Dakota, he'd be thrown from his horse, crack a bone, climb into the saddle again, and go on rounding up cattle.

He says that he developed courage by doing the things he was afraid to do—by acting as if he were brave even though he were half scared to death. He finally became so courageous he didn't fear even roaring lions or blazing cannon.

During the Bull Moose campaign in 1912, a half-crazy man shot Roosevelt in the breast while he was on his way to make a speech. Roosevelt didn't let anybody know that the bullet had struck him. He went right on to the auditorium and started to speak and kept on speaking until he almost collapsed from loss of blood. Then he was rushed to the hospital.

When he was in the White House, he slept with a loaded revolver by his pillow, and he carried a small pistol whenever he went out for a walk.

While he was President, he was boxing with an army officer. The soldier hit him squarely in the left eye, broke the blood vessels, and permanently injured his sight. Roosevelt didn't want the young man to realize what he had done; so when the officer asked him to box again, the President said no, he guessed he was getting too old to box. Years later, he lost the sight of that eye completely, but he never let the captain of artillery know what had happened.

He chopped all the firewood used on his estate at Oyster Bay, pitched hay in the field with the farm hands, and insisted on his gardener's paying him the same wages he paid the rest of the help.

He never smoked, he never swore, and about the only drinking he ever did was to take a teaspoonful of brandy, on rare occasions, in a milk-shake at night. He didn't even know there was any brandy in the milk-shake until his valet told him about it; yet he was called a hard drinker so often that he finally had to bring a libel suit to stop the slander.

Busy as he was, he found time to read hundreds and hundreds of books while he was in the White House. He would often have the entire forenoon packed tight with a series of five-minute interviews; but he kept a book by his side to utilize even the few spare seconds that elapsed between his callers.

When he went traveling, he usually carried a pocket edition of Shakespeare or Bobbie Burns. Once when he was punching cattle in Dakota, he sat beside a flickering campfire and read the whole of *Hamlet* aloud to a cowboy. On his trip through the jungles of Brazil, he spent his evenings reading Gibbons' *Decline and Fall of the Roman Empire*.

He loved music, but he couldn't carry a tune himself. While he was working alone, he often tried to sing *Nearer My God To Thee*. Once he rode through the streets of a western town, tipping his hat to the cheering throngs, and all the while, he kept singing to himself *Nearer My God To Thee*.

He had many hobbies. Once, when he was in the White House, he telephoned a well-known Washington newspaper correspondent to come to the Executive Mansion at once. This newspaper reporter, excited by the request, imagined he was going to have an exclusive interview about some affair of state; so he wired his paper to hold the presses ready to dash off an extra immediately.

When the reporter arrived at the White House, Roosevelt didn't say a word about politics, instead, he led the reporter out to an old hollow tree in the White House yard and showed him a nest of young owls he had discovered.

On a train trip through the West at one time, he was talking to a group of executives in his private car. Suddenly he saw a farmer standing in his corn field beside the tracks, with his hat off. Roosevelt knew the man was paying his respects to the President of the United States; so he jumped up, rushed to the rear platform, and waved his hat furiously. He didn't do that as a political stunt. He did it because deep in his heart, he liked people.

During the last year of his life, his health began to fail, and, although he was only sixty, he remarked several times that he was getting old. He wrote a letter to an aged friend saying: "You and I are within reach of the rifle pits, and any moment we may go down into the darkness."

He died peacefully in his sleep. on January 4, 1919. The last words he ever uttered were: "Please put out the lights."

WOODROW WILSON

HE WAS FACED WITH ONE OF
THE GREATEST OPPORTUNITIES IN HISTORY:
YET HE FAILED BECAUSE HE COULDN'T HANDLE PEOPLE

WHAT KIND OF man was the real Woodrow Wilson?

He has been called a supreme genius; he has also been called a magnificent failure.

He saw a vision of world peace —the League of Nations —and on the altar of that vision, he consecrated every ounce of his vitality and his strength-finally he died, a man shattered by his own ideal.

When Woodrow Wilson sailed for Europe in

1919, he was called the savior of the ages. Bleeding Europe hailed him as a god. Starving peasants burned candles before his picture and offered up prayers to him as though he were a saint.

The whole world lay at his feet. Yet when he returned to this country three months later, a sick and broken man, he had alienated many friends and made a hundred million enemies.

History presents Woodrow Wilson as an idealistic school-teacher—cold, dignified, and lacking in human warmth. Yet the truth is almost exactly the opposite. Wilson was intensely human—hungry for human relationships—and it was the sorrow of his life that his own shyness kept him aloof and apart.

"I would give anything in the world if I were different," he said, "but I cannot make myself over."

Sometimes he could unbend. When he was a professor at Wesleyan University, he jumped down out of the bleachers one day and led the cheering at a football game. And when he was in Bermuda, he went sailing for the sheer pleasure of chatting with the Negro boatmen.

Woodrow Wilson was probably the most scholarly man who ever sat in the White House, yet he couldn't read or write until he was eleven years old. His favorite reading for relaxation was detective stories.

He cared little for art. He often said that he would rather have a chromo that you can buy in a ten cent store than a Whistler etching.

And this highbrow professor who had spent his life in the cloistered atmosphere of academies frankly said that he would rather see a musical comedy than a Shakespearian play. He said he didn't go to the theatre to be edified. He went there to be entertained—and when he was in the White House, he went to vaudeville shows almost every week.

Most of his life he had been poor. His salary as a

teacher was so small that his wife painted pictures and sold them to help support the family.

As a young professor, Woodrow Wilson couldn't afford to buy good clothes; and later in life, like Lincoln, he cared little about his personal appearance. For example, when he was President, his valet urged him to send his old dress-suit to the tailor to have the lapels re-faced with new satin; but Woodrow Wilson said, "No, don't bother. That is good for a year yet."

And like Lincoln, Wilson was indifferent to food. He ate whatever was set before him and often seemed to be unconscious of what he was eating.

He smoked only one cigar in his life—or rather, he didn't smoke all of even one, for he got sick before he finished it.

His only extravagance was buying beautiful books.

Under his frozen exterior, Woodrow Wilson was a

man of quick and fierce emotion. Those who knew him said he had a hotter temper than Theodore Roosevelt. His devotion to his first wife was intense and pathetic. One of his first acts after he became President was to buy his wife a set of sable furs. When she died a year later, he would not permit her body to be removed from the White House for seventy-two hours. He had it laid on a sofa, and for three days and three nights, he would not leave her side.

He was regarded as an intellectual giant; but he had little command of languages, he was unacquainted with much of the world's great literature, he was indifferent to science, and he cared very little for philosophy.

He started out in life to be a lawyer, but at law he was a dismal failure. He never conducted a case by himself in his life, and he handled property for only one client—his mother.

Probably the greatest flaw in Wilson's character was his lack of tact. The ambition of his whole life, from his boyhood on, was to become a statesman. He practiced public speaking in his room for hours at a time. In order to perfect himself, he did futile things, for example, he even posted a chart on his wall showing how to make appropriate gestures. But he overlooked the most important thing of all—he never learned how to handle people. The last years of his life were a tragic series of broken friendships. He quarreled with the leaders of the senate. He broke off with his closest friends such as colonel House. Finally, he alienated many of the people of his own country by asking them to elect only Democrats to office.

When the Senate refused to accept the League of Nations, Wilson appealed directly to the people. His health had always been delicate and his physicians warned him against any additional strain. But he ignored their advice.

During the last year of the Presidency, this intellectual genius whose words had once shaken the world, was now so broken and weak that he couldn't sign his own name without someone guiding his hand.

After his retirement, people came from all over the world to his house on S Street in Washington — came to as though it were a shrine. And when he lay dying, pilgrims knelt on the pavement before his house and prayed for the passing of his soul.

JACK LONDON

THE "TOUGH GUY" WHO WENT THROUGH
HIGH SCHOOL IN THREE MONTHS
AND WROTE FIFTY-ONE BOOKS IN EIGHTEEN YEARS

∽ A LITTLE OVER fifty years ago, a hobo rode the rods of a freight train into Buffalo and began to beg for food from door to door. A policeman arrested him for vagrancy, and a judge sentenced him to thirty days at hard labor in the penitentiary. For thirty days, he broke rocks and had nothing whatever to eat except bread and water.

Yet six years later—only six years later, mind you, this hobo, this former bum and panhandler, was the most sought-after man on the Western coast. He was entertained by the cream of California society and hailed by novelists, critics, and editors, as one of the brightest stars on the literary horizon.

He never went to high school until he was nineteen, and he died when he was forty; but he left behind him fifty-one books.

He was Jack London, author of *The Call of the Wild*.

When Jack London wrote *The Call of the Wild* back in 1903, he became famous overnight. Editors clamored for his work. But he made very little money from his first big hit. The publishers—and later the movie producers in Hollywood—made a million dollars out of it; but he himself sold all his rights to *The Call of the Wild* for only two thousand dollars.

If you want to write a book, the very first requisite is to have something to write about. That was one of the secrets of Jack London's astonishing success. He packed ten thousand colorful experiences into his short and feverish life. He was a sailor before the mast, a longshoreman, an oyster-pirate, and a gold miner. He hunted seals in the far North. He hoboed over half the earth, and wrote a book about his experiences as a tramp.

He often went hungry. He slept on park benches and in hay stacks and box cars. He often slept on the hard ground—and sometimes woke up and found himself sleeping in a pool of water. He was so exhausted at times that he fell asleep while riding the rods underneath a freight train.

He was arrested and thrown into jails hundreds of times here in America and he was clamped into the jails of Mexico, Manchuria, Japan and Korea.

Jack London's childhood was seared with poverty and hardships. He ran wild with a gang of hoodlums who roamed the water-front along San Francisco

Bay. School? He laughed at schools and played hookey most of the time. Yet one day he wandered into a public library and began reading *Robinson Crusoe*. He was fascinated. Hungry as he was, he didn't even stop to run home for supper. The next day, he rushed back to the library to read other books. A new world was opening up before him—a world as strange and colorful as the Bagdad of the *Arabian Nights*.

From that time on, he had an unquenchable passion for books. He often read ten and fifteen hours a day. He devoured everything from Nick Carter to Shakespeare—everything from Herbert Spencer to Karl Marx.

When he was nineteen, he decided to stop selling his muscles and sell his brain instead. He was tired of hoboing, tired of being beaten up by policemen, tired of having railroad brakemen hit him over the head with their lanterns.

So, at the age of nineteen, he entered high school in Oakland, California. He studied night and day, took hardly any time at all for sleep and did a phenomenal thing. He actually crammed four years of work into three months, passed his examinations, and then entered the University of California.

Obsessed with a driving ambition to become a great writer, he studied *Treasure Island*, *The Count of Monte Cristo*, and *The Tale of Two Cities*—studied them over and over and then wrote feverishly. He wrote five thousand words a day, that means a full length novel in twenty days. He sometimes had thirty stories out in the hands of editors at the same time. But they all came back. He was merely learning his trade.

Then one day one of his stories entitled *Typhoon Off the Coast of Japan* won first prize in a contest sponsored by the *San Francisco Call*. He got only twenty dollars for the story. He was broke, and couldn't pay even his room rent.

That was 1896—a year of drama and excitement. Gold was discovered in the Klondike. Telegraph wires flashed the sensational news across the continent and thrilled the nation.

Workmen left their shops, soldiers deserted from the army, farmers abandoned their lands, merchants locked their stores. The gold-diggers were on the move. The locust swarm of humanity took wings and headed for the golden land under the northern lights.

And Jack London was with them. He spent a hectic year hunting for gold in the Klondike. He endured incredible hardships. Eggs were worth twenty-five cents apiece and butter sold for three dollars a pound. He slept on the ground with the thermometer at 74 degrees below zero. Finally he drifted back to the States without a penny in his pocket.

He did whatever odd jobs he could find. He washed dishes in restaurants. He scrubbed floors. He worked on the docks and in factories.

Then one day, with only two dollars between himself and hunger, he decided to give up manual labor forever and devote all of his time to literature. That was in 1898. Five years later, in 1903, he had published six books and one hundred and twenty-five short stories, and was one of the most talked-of men in literary America.

Jack London died in 1916, only eighteen years after he really started to write, and during that time, he wrote an average of about three books a year besides countless stories.

And his yearly income was twice as much as the President of the United States. His books are still enormously popular and in Europe, he is one of the most widely read of all American authors.

The Call of the Wild, for which he got only two

thousand dollars, has been translated into a score of languages. It has sold more than a million and a half copies and is one of the most popular books in the history of American literature.

CHIC SALE

HE GOT $49.49 A WORD—FOR A BOOK
HE WAS SORRY HE EVER WROTE!

THERE HAS BEEN only one author in the history of the world who ever wrote a book and made $49.49 profit on every single word in the book. That book was *The Specialist*, and its author was Chic Sale.

The Specialist was the first book Chic Sale ever wrote, and he had so little faith in it that he printed only two thousand copies at first; and it took six weeks to sell them.

Then suddenly the book caught on and swept over

the country like flames leaping and roaring through a pine forest. It sold more copies than *The Good Earth*!

You'd think, wouldn't you, that an author would be mighty proud of writing a book that outsold *The Good Earth?* But Chic Sale wasn't. He regretted that he ever wrote *The Specialist*—regretted it because its humor has been misunderstood by many people.

On the other hand, he was proud of the success it achieved. He was embarrassed when people spoke of the book in his presence, and preferred that no one mention it, especially if he thought the person considered the humor vulgar. Once his daughter actually wept because she felt the book had disgraced the family.

Chic Sale became an author more or less by accident. Actually, he was an actor and one of the finest character actors that ever put on grease paint.

For that matter, he became an actor more or less by accident too. Years ago, he was a mechanic, working in the railroad shops in Urbana, Illinois. His older sister had stage aspirations, so she went to Chicago and studied at a dramatic school. When she came home for Christmas vacation she gave a program at one of the churches and mimicked country characters.

After her performance was over, Chic said, "Why, I can do that without going to school."

She dared him to, so he walked out in the middle of the floor and gave an imitation of the local telegraph operator in Urbana. In a few minutes, he had the natives almost rolling off their chairs.

The next week a troupe of actors came to Urbana to put on a show. They had a comedy man who came out between the acts and entertained the audience, but he got sick. Chic Sale heard about it, and applied for the job.

The manager of the show was skeptical. But Chic gave him a sample of what he could do, and the manager took him on for the week, paid him ten dollars, and changed Chic's whole life.

Footlights! Glamor! The laughter of five hundred people! The applause of an audience! Why, a log chain and a span of Missouri mules couldn't have dragged him back to the machine shop after that.

Packing up his old telescope suitcase, he dashed off to Chicago, got a job on the stage and went to a cheap rooming house and began rehearsing his stunt. He decided that whiskers would make him look more like an old man; but he didn't know where he could buy them, so he took some hair stuffing out of his mattress, and made himself a set of whiskers out of horsehair.

He used these mattress whiskers on the stage for eight months before he bought a real set of whiskers from a dealer in theatrical make-up.

His pay was very small, and every penny was precious. In order to keep himself from eating too much, he would buy cheap candy and nibble on it awhile before dinner. This, most of the time, took the edge off his appetite.

Something hurt his stomach. Maybe it was this cheap candy. At any rate, he spent thousands of dollars for operations, and he carried a cook with him wherever he went because he couldn't eat hotel cooking.

He also carried a steel trunk with him, a trunk made into a filing cabinet and filled with thousands of jokes! He had one of the world's largest collections of jokes, but he never told a funny story in a private conversation.

He played in six musical comedies on Broadway; but he couldn't sing and he couldn't dance. He was the best known "horn player" in the United States; yet he couldn't play a horn. He made $50,000 playing in shows that were about Paris; yet he never saw Paris.

He wore the same pair of shoes on the stage for sixteen years. They were the shoes he used when he played the parts of old men. He believed they brought him good luck, so he kept on repairing them and refused to have any others.

While playing in vaudeville, he fell in love with a girl from Missoula, Montana, an enchanting creature crowned with an aura of moonlight and flowering jasmine.

He wasn't scared in the least when he faced a thousand people, in the theatre; but when he tried to propose to his girl, he stuttered and blushed and felt miserable. Saying he was ill, he left her and went to his hotel room.

When he got there, he proposed to her over the telephone. She accepted, they were married, and had four Children.

After making so much money out of *The Specialist*, Chic Sale wrote another book. It was called: *The Corn Husker Crashes the Movies* and it didn't bring in enough cash to pay the printing bills!

FRANCIS YEATS-BROWN

WHAT THE MOVIES DIDN'T TELL ABOUT
THE BENGAL LANCER

ONE AFTERNOON a slim, serious young Englishman by the name of Yeats-Brown sat before my fireplace in Forest Hills and kept me spellbound for hours with tales of his adventures in the mystic and fabled lands of the East. He was thirty-nine years old then; and ever since he was nineteen, he had seen death on many battlefields.

He had been a prisoner of war in Bagdad and Constantinople. He had fought the Turks on the scorching hot desert sands of Mesopotamia, and he had fought the Germans on the muddy fields of Flanders.

He had written a book entitled *The Bloody Years*, and yet, like Lawrence of Arabia, I found him a quiet, soft-spoken English gentleman more interested in poetry and philosophy than in fighting.

Yeats-Brown had little money to show for his twenty years of soldiering. He had no idea what the future held in store for him. But he didn't seem very much worried. Out there in the East, he had learned something of the calm philosophy of the Orient. He had become a disciple of mysticism and Yoga; he had studied under holy men and sought the secrets of the Vedanta.

He hadn't lived just one life like most of us. In his thirty-nine years, he had lived many lives—in fact, when he finally wrote the story of his hectic career in which he related many of the things he told me that afternoon, he called the book, *The Lives of a Bengal Lancer*. It was the sensational success of 1930. And it made one of the most engrossing films that ever came out of Hollywood. But, like most Hollywood films based on biographies, it deviated very, very far from the facts of Yeats-Brown's astonishing career.

Francis Yeats-Brown was only nineteen years old when he first put on the dashing blue and gold uniform and the blue and gold turban of the Royal Bengal Lancers—the proudest and lordliest cavalry in all the far-flung dominions of His Britannic Majesty.

They were a picked body of men, the crack regiment of India, these Bengal Lancers. Their pay was almost nothing—something like ten dollars a month—and they had to supply their own horses and their own equipment. But they didn't go out there to Mother India for gain, these daring young men of

England. They went there for glory—went out there embued with the spirit that carried Kitchener and Chinese Gordon and Sir Francis Drake and Sir Walter Raleigh to the ends of the earth.

They were up every morning at five o'clock and drilled for hours until the sun rose in the sky and the barrels of their guns became so hot they couldn't hold them any longer.

And, with the thermometer sizzling at one hundred degrees in the shade, they found their recreation tearing up and down the polo field. They were cut down by sun stroke and their bodies racked with malaria.

But Yeats-Brown told me that the most dangerous and exciting sport in all India was "pig-sticking." That's what the English call it—"pig-sticking." Actually, it's galloping through forests of brambles and over rough, stony country hunting a wild boar with nothing but a bamboo pole with a spear stuck in the end of it.

No other animal in the world is so vicious as a wild boar that has been wounded. Three hundred pounds of bristling fury, sly as a fox, courageous as a lion, and as fast on his trotters as the swiftest cavalry horse. To fall within range of his razor-sharp tusks, means quick and certain death.

I asked Yeats-Brown to tell me of his narrowest escape from death. He said it occurred one day while he was out "pig-sticking." He and his men had flushed a great boar out of the brambles. The savage pig was racing across the field, his huge tusks glistening in the sun.

Yeats-Brown, mounted on his polo pony, was in hot pursuit. Just as he drove his spear into the pig, his horse stumbled; and horse, pig and Yeats-Brown went down in a screaming, whinnying, helpless mass of tangled legs and clawing forefeet. Yeats-Brown was pinned under his kicking horse; the pig, impaled upon the spear was struggling to get up. The horse heaved. And the pig got loose just as Yeats-Brown leaped to his feet and tore for the nearest tree. There he sat until a rescue party rode up. He had lost a tooth, sprained a thumb, and was bruised and mashed from head to foot. The pig was dead from his wounds.

The only one who was completely happy was the horse, who ambled about nibbling grass with the unhurried leisure of the East.

But I suppose the strangest episode in Yeats-Brown's strange career was the time he disguised himself as a woman. He had been fighting the Turks out in Mesopotamia or "Mespot" as he called it. He had been taken prisoner by the Turks and had escaped from his vermin-infested cell in Constantinople, but had not been able to get out of the city. The Turkish authorities were searching for him frantically.

Naturally they were looking for an English officer, so they never suspected a German governess who used to meet a Russian prince in one of the cafés. The Russian prince was also being watched by the authorities, but the sentimental Turks hadn't the heart to interfere with a little harmless flirtation. So when Yeats-Brown, all dolled up as a German governess, in a picture hat, with a veil, a black fox scarf around his shoulders and a muff over his hands, minced into the café, the Russian prince would jump to his feet, bow respectfully and kiss the lady's hand.

And the Turkish detectives would smile at one another knowingly and shrug their shoulders. After all, even a suspect Russian prince was entitled to a little romance.

He was unable to get out of Turkey disguised as Mademoiselle Josephine, so he played another role. Overnight, he changed his sex and nationality and became a Hungarian mechanic who had lost his job in a munitions factory. He grew a small turned-up mustache and wore a derby hat, a pair of steel-rimmed glasses, a stained white vest, and a pair of shoes with elastic sides. Actually he looked like a second-rate comedian, but the Turks never doubted that he was the real McCoy.

Finally he was caught and thrown back into prison again. Once more he escaped by passing himself off as one of a crowd of Greeks who ate their supper in the prison garden. When they went out he went out with them, and walked down the street as calm and serene as the ever-living Buddha.

I asked him what was the most terrible sight he ever saw in all his years of fighting, and he told me this story. When he was a prisoner of war, the Turks forced him to march two hundred miles to a prison camp; on the way, he marched through a town where there wasn't a single living inhabitant. The Turkish army had butchered a whole village of Armenians. The silence of death was everywhere, and the only living creatures were a few dogs slinking through the silent streets and the buzzards circling in the sky overhead.

AL JOLSON

ONCE DOOMED TO DIE FOR WANT OF TEN CENTS—HE LIVED TO TEAR UP $1,000,000.

◠ SO FAR AS I KNOW, there is only one actor in America who ever tore up a contract worth a million dollars.

You have seen him in pictures, you have sung his songs, you have laughed at his jokes. He made the first full-length talking picture. And he also made the greatest box-office attraction that was ever created in Hollywood—a picture that earned twelve million dollars, an all-time record that has never been approached by any other film.

That picture was *The Singing Fool*, and the man who starred in it was Asa Yoelson—Al Jolson to you.

Jolson once drew a salary of $31,250 a week and he drew it for more than six months without doing a day's work. That means he was paid almost a million dollars for doing absolutely nothing. To be sure, he was ready to perform; but his employers, United Artists, had no script ready to shoot just then; so he played golf and collected a salary that made the income of the President of the United States look like a stenographer's stipend.

Then he did one of the most unexpected and generous acts that has ever brightened the cynical darkness of Hollywood. The depression had just struck. Joseph Schenck, a life-long friend of Jolson's, had lost heavily. There was still more than a million dollars due Al Jolson on his contract; but he tore the contract up and handed it back to Joseph

Schenck, head of United Artists, saying: "Forget it! I'm not doing anything for you and you don't need to pay me any more money."

Charles Schwab once created a sensation in Wall Street by tearing up a salary contract that guaranteed him a million dollars a year; but this once-poor actor tore up a contract that was paying him almost two million dollars a year. Nobody asked him to do it; nobody expected him to do it.

Al Jolson had tuberculosis when he was a boy. When he went to a free clinic at Bellevue Hospital for treatment, the doctors told him that if he didn't get away to the country at once, he would be dead in six months. The prescription they gave him was free, so was the medicine; but when he went to get it, he discovered that he had to pay ten cents for a bottle. He didn't have a dime—so to this day, he has never got the medicine.

He recovered without it, anyhow—and without

the doctors. But he has never forgotten how it felt to be doomed to die because he didn't have ten cents. That is why he now spends twenty thousand dollars a year supporting free beds for poor people in a tuberculosis sanitarium in the Adirondacks at Saranac Lake. He has been doing this for eleven years; and he has never seen half of the people whose lives he has saved.

I'm often curious about people's birthdays; but when I asked Al Jolson when he was born, he said he didn't know. He was born of poor parents in Russia, born in a little hut with a straw roof and a stone floor. One year was about like another, and his parents didn't bother to keep track of a little thing like the birth of a child. So he hasn't the remotest idea whether he was born in 1885 or 1886 or 1888. But after he became famous, his friends wanted to give him birthday presents, so he had to pick out a birthday. He knew it would be bad business to be born in the autumn, for actors are always broke at the beginning of a season. But they are usually feeling pretty flush in the spring, and since May is a nice, warm month, he decided to be born in May—May 26, 1888. He admits that date is not accurate, but it is near enough. Anyhow, it can't be more than four or five years out of the way.

Jolson got his first job on the stage when he was a child—a small part in a play called *Children of the Ghetto*. He had just one line—he had to rush on to the stage and shout: "Kill the Jews!"

His father had a job just then slaughtering cattle in a kosher butcher shop during the week and singing in the synagogue on the Sabbath. So when he heard that his son was shouting in the theatre, "Kill the Jews!" young Jolson's career almost came to an abrupt end.

When Jolson first came to New York, he was penniless, and had to steal a ride from Washington.

He was so unsophisticated that when he got to Newark, New Jersey, he thought he was in New York City; so he got off the train and had to sleep that night in a thicket of grass in the Jersey Meadows. When he awoke, his legs and hands were a mass of mosquito bites—raw, swollen, and bleeding.

When he finally got to New York, he slept on park benches and on trucks down by the water front. For days he went hungry. The best he could hope for then was a chance to "jump for nickels" in some Bowery saloon.

Lee Shubert once remarked that there were only two legitimate actors in America who could go into any big town and fill a theatre on the strength of their names alone. One was Fred Stone, and the other was Al Jolson.

Yet Al Jolson told me that the first time he ever appeared at the Winter Garden, he was heartbroken.

It was a long show, and he didn't go on until after midnight. He got no applause. Nothing. Not a ripple. That night, after the curtain was rung down, he stumbled up Broadway, sick with discouragement. He lived on Fifty-fourth Street, but he was so dazed that he walked all the way to Ninetieth Street—forty-six blocks out of his way—before he realized where he was!

And the furthest thing from his thoughts at that moment—from even his most delirious dreams—was that some day his name would flash like an aurora over Broadway, and that managers would leap at the chance of paying him ten dollars a minute!

SINCLAIR LEWIS

FIRED FROM FOUR NEWSPAPERS—HE
WON THE NOBEL PRIZE AND THOUGHT IT WAS A GAG

MY FIRST ENCOUNTER with Sinclair Lewis was years back. Years ago, he and I and a half-dozen other chaps used to hire a motor boat at Freeport, Long Island, and chug out a few miles to fish for mackerel or weakfish. In those days, I took my hat off to Red Lewis because he never got seasick. The waves would toss and the sea would pitch, and down I would go to the bottom of the boat; but Lewis just sat up straight and kept on fishing like a man on a painted ocean.

Today I take my hat off to Sinclair Lewis, not for his skill as a fisherman (I can stay on deck myself now) but because he has written an unceasing stream of excellent novels. And if you don't think that's a man's job—try it!

Sinclair Lewis hit the bull's eye for the first time in 1920. Previous to that, he had written six books without causing a literary ripple. His seventh novel was *Main Street* and it swept over the nation like a tornado. Women's clubs condemned it, preachers denounced it, and newspapers called it an insult to American life. It raised a veritable literary war here; and the repercussions of it were heard three thousand miles away in Europe.

That book made him a literary star of the first magnitude.

Some of the critics said: "Well, that's fine; but that smart aleck will never be able to do it again."

Oh, no?

The red-headed boy from Sauk Center, Minnesota, set to work; and since then he has—well, I was about to say he has "dashed" off half a dozen best sellers. But Sinclair Lewis doesn't dash off his books. He works over them, constantly revising and rewriting.

He wrote an outline of sixty thousand words for his novel *Arrowsmith*. That means that the mere outline was more than half as long as the average novel. He worked for twelve months once on a novel about capital and labor and then tossed the manuscript into the wastepaper basket.

He started to write *Main Street* three different times. He started it exactly seventeen years before he finished it.

Main Street was followed by a whole series of books that leaped instantly into the best-seller class. *Babbitt — Arrowsmith — Elmer Gantry — Dodsworth —Ann Vickers —It Can't Happen Here....*

I once asked Sinclair Lewis to tell me the most astonishing fact he knew about himself. He thought a moment and then said that if he weren't doing literary work, he would prefer either to teach Greek or Philosophy in Oxford University—or go out to the deep woods and live with a bunch of lumber jacks.

For six months out of the year, he loves to live on swanky Park Avenue; but during the other six months, he lives in an isolated spot in the Vermont mountains, eighty miles southeast of Burlington. He has a three-hundred-and-forty-acre farm up there covered with sugar trees and he makes his own maple syrup and raises his own vegetables. And he "goes in to town" only when he needs a hair-cut.

I asked, "Red, how does it feel to be famous?"—and he replied, "Oh, it's a nuisance." He told me that if he answered all his mail. he not only would never be able to write another book, but he wouldn't even have time to sleep. So he just chucks most of his letters into the fire-place and watches them burn.

He dislikes autograph hunters, seldom goes to public dinners, and shuns literary teas.

When I began talking about his early struggles, he said, "Oh, these writers that are always talking about their early struggles give me a pain. The trouble with most American writers is that they don't have enough struggles. They don't have any more trouble getting started than do young dentists and doctors and lawyers; but they are more articulate and they like to talk about what a hard time they have had."

I reminded him of the fact that for years he used to get up a couple of hours before breakfast and go out to the kitchen and put the coffee on to boil and write on the kitchen table. I reminded him that he once borrowed a hundred and fifty dollars and did his own cooking and washing and worked night and day for six months, and the only thing that he sold during all that time was one joke for two dollars. But he said there was no hardship to that, he said he was merely learning his trade and he never had a better time in his life than he did during those years.

I asked him how many copies of his books had been sold, and he said he didn't know. I said, "Well, now, come, you can give me even an approximate figure, can't you?" And he said, "No, I haven't the slightest idea."

I asked him how much money he made out of *Main Street*. He told me that he didn't know and he really didn't care. He said he had an attorney and an accountant to look after his business affairs, and he never paid any attention to how much money he was making.

He has had all sorts of experiences. His father was a country doctor on the prairies of Minnesota and Sinclair Lewis sometimes gave a patient chloroform while his father performed an operation. He once worked his way across the Atlantic Ocean on a cattle boat and he once traveled in the steerage down to Panama to get a job. He used to write children's poetry, he used to sell plots for stories to Jack London, and he used to be assistant-editor of a magazine for deaf people.

He doesn't take any exercise whatever. He agrees with George Jean Nathan that opening the door of a taxicab and crawling inside is all the exercise a city man needs.

He has no interest whatever in sports. Babe Ruth is the only baseball player he can name, and Red Grange is the only football player he ever heard of.

"You were fired from the first three newspapers you worked for, weren't you?" I asked.

"No. I was fired from the first *four* papers I worked for," was his reply.

I wanted to ask him what advice he would give to young writers and I began, "What advice...." and he said—"None." He doesn't believe in giving anybody any advice about anything.

One day somebody with a Swedish accent telephoned him saying that he had been awarded the Nobel Prize for literature. Sinclair Lewis had known a lot of Swedes out in Minnesota, and he thought this fellow's accent was a bit phony; Red supposed some friend was playing a joke on him and he began to kid the fellow.

A few minutes later, Lewis was flabbergasted when he discovered that it was all real—that he really had won the greatest distinction in the literary world!

DIAMOND JIM BRADY

HE OFFERED A MILLION DOLLARS FOR A BRIDE

◦ DIAMOND JIM BRADY, the Haroun Al Raschid of Broadway, died during the first World War; and his passing robbed the Great White Way of one of its most incredible phenomena. While he lived, Brady threw the wildest parties this weary old world has seen since the days when the old Roman Emperors dined on the nightingales' tongues. Sometimes he had as many as five parties whooping it up all at once in five different parts of the town. Sometimes these parties lasted for seventeen riotous hours, and cost as high as a hundred thousand dollars. He was fond of presenting his guests with souvenirs to take home with them—little knick-knacks and mementoes, such as diamond brooches or diamond watches worth a thousand dollars apiece.

Diamond Jim, the Good-time Charlie of Broadway, was born in a cheap flat above a saloon which his father kept on the waterfront in New York; he learned to pop the cork out of a bottle before he learned his *Mother Goose*. Yet he himself never drank a drop of liquor in his life. During the years when he reigned supreme on Broadway, he squandered hundreds of dollars on liquor, buying more champagne and Rhine wine than any other man in the Western Hemisphere, but he gave it all to his friends. While they drank themselves under the table, Diamond Jim sat by and quenched *his* inconsequential thirst on fourteen or fifteen steins of root beer.

He weighed two hundred and fifty pounds, and loved to eat. He devoured a fifteen-course dinner every night with usually two or three helpings of all the main courses. Then he would eat a pound of chocolates and take a box of peppermints along to the theatre. He sent hundreds of boxes of candy to his friends each week. His candy bill alone averaged between two and three thousand dollars a month. He detested tea and coffee, but he had a passion for orange juice. He drank a whole gallon of orange juice before he even tucked a napkin under his bottommost chin, and he often guzzled another whole gallon with his meal. Once he ate six chickens at one sitting. This sounds fantastic, but in his old age, when he underwent an operation, the doctors discovered that he had a stomach six times the normal size.

How did Diamond Jim Brady make his millions?

He was one of the most expert salesmen that this high-pressure country ever produced. Besides, he was lucky. He got the breaks. He started selling steel cars in the early days when the railroads were equipped with wooden coaches. The country was expanding. Railroads were being flung like lariats from ocean to ocean and from Canada to the Gulf.

When he first started selling steel cars, they were still an experiment. No one wanted them. So he was given what turned out to be a phenomenal contract. This contract gave him 33 1/3%commission on every car sold. Presently every railroad in the nation was clamoring for steel cars. And they had to come, hat in hand, to Diamond Jim Brady to get them, for at that time he had no competitors. So he made twelve million dollars selling steel cars. He was a product of his age. If he had been born fifty years later and tried selling steel cars today, he might not have been able to pay his grocery bill.

Diamond Jim made himself famous from Skowhegan to Santa Fé by one of the weirdest publicity stunts ever heard of since the days of Barnum. He literally *bedecked* himself with diamonds. He owned a different set of jewelry for every day in the month, and he frequently changed his jewelry as often as six or seven times a day. He used to ramble down Broadway bespangled with no less than two thousand, five hundred and forty-eight scintillating diamonds —and nineteen rubies. He wore priceless shirt-studs made to represent bicycles and automobiles, and cuff-links made like locomotives and freight cars.

He went to preposterous lengths to spend his money. He had a farm in New Jersey where, on gala occasions, the cows were milked into pails heavily plated with gold. His billiard table was inlaid with carnelians and lapis lazuli. His poker chips were made of onyx and mother-of-pearl. He paid an interior-decorator a third of a million dollars to furnish his house, and every year he gave away all his furniture to his friends and bought himself new furnishings.

He presented Lillian Russell with a bicycle plated with gold and studded all over with hundreds of diamonds, rubies, sapphires and emeralds. And when the shapely Lillian pedaled *that* bike up Fifth Avenue—well, things happened to the traffic!

Diamond Jim owned five thousand handkerchiefs and two hundred suits of clothes, and he never permitted himself to be seen in public without a Prince Albert and a tall silk hat. Even if he was only riding a handcar down a stretch of Western track with no one but prairie dogs to see him, Diamond Jim still wore his Prince Albert coat and his stovepipe hat and carried his diamond-studded cane.

If Diamond Jim's stomach was six times its normal size, so was his heart. For years, he lent money with a lavish hand to almost everyone who came to him with a hard-luck story. He knew he would never get most of it back, but he didn't mind. "It's fun to be a sucker," he said, " —if you can afford it."

When he knew that he was going to die, he discovered that he held notes and I.O.U.'s for a fifth of a million dollars; and one of the last things he ever did was to destroy every note in his possession, just to make sure that his executors wouldn't try to collect them.

"If I'm gonna die," he said, "I'm gonna die. But I ain't gonna leave trouble and heartache behind me."

When he died, he left practically all of his great fortune to charity. His diamonds and rubies and emeralds were estimated to be worth two million dollars. These were taken out of their settings and put into rings and sold again; so that many a woman today, without suspecting it, is wearing a stone that once enhanced the expansive charms of Diamond Jim.

Everyone "loved" Diamond Jim, yet he always remained a bachelor. He laid a million dollars in Lillian Russell's lap and asked her to marry him, but she refused. And once he said, "There ain't a woman in the world would marry an ugly-lookin' guy like me," and he laid his head on the table and cried like a baby.

HETTY GREEN

SHE RESOLD HER MORNING PAPER AND
SPENT HOURS IN THE JULY SUN SORTING RAGS,
TO INCREASE HER FORTUNE OF $65,000,000.

AT ONE TIME, Hetty Green was the richest woman in America. At her death, she was worth at least $65,000,000 — possibly $100,000,000. Yet almost any scrubwoman wears finer clothes than Hetty Green wore, eats a better dinner, and sleeps in a better bed.

Her income was $5. a minute, or $300 an hour; yet she would buy a morning newspaper for two cents, read it, and then have it sold again.

On cold winter days, she often padded herself

with newspapers to keep warm. She bought a couple of railroads outright—bought them lock, stock, and barrel—and she owned bonds of almost every railroad in the country; yet when she was taking a train journey, she never indulged in the luxury of a Pullman berth, but sat up all night in the day coach.

Once she invited her friends to meet her at the Parker House in Boston for a dinner party. Everyone expected it to be quite an affair. Ladies appeared in their evening wraps, and the gentlemen wore dinner coats. But after her guests had arrived, Hetty led them out of the hotel and walked them a long distance to a cheap boarding house and treated them to a twenty-five cent dinner.

Sometimes when she was in Boston, she ate at a restaurant in Pie Alley—a place where one could get a plate of beans for three cents and a small wedge of pie for two cents. Her income then was more than eight cents every second. That meant she would have had to eat four pieces of pie every second just to keep up with her income.

When she was seventy-eight years old, a newspaper reporter asked her the secret of her good health. She said that she ate a tenderloin steak, fried potatoes, a cup of tea and some milk every morning for breakfast and then chewed baked onions all day to kill the germs that were in the steak and the milk. Unfortunately, she didn't say what she chewed to kill the germs in the onions.

On a sizzling hot day in 1893, Hetty Green crawled up into the attic of a warehouse that she had inherited from her father. The July sun boiled down upon the iron roof and made the attic just a trifle less hot than the outskirts of Hades. Yet Hetty Green worked in that devastating heat for hours.... Doing what?.... Sorting white rags from colored ones because the junk man paid a cent a pound more for white rags!

She had to spend most of her time in Wall Street looking after her investments. That was dangerous, and she knew it. She realized that if she rented an apartment in New York City, or owned even one stick of furniture in the state, the tax collector would swoop down upon her and take $30,000 from her every year. So, to dodge tax collectors, she drifted about from one cheap lodging house to another. Even her best friends didn't know where she was hiding half the time. She lived under assumed names, dressed in rags, and carried so little baggage that suspicious landladies often made her pay for her night's lodging in advance.

As she grew older, a miracle happened. A friend persuaded her to spend $300 for beauty treatments. Each treatment was guaranteed to make her look one year younger.

Always fearing that some crook would forge her signature to a check, she never signed her name unless she had to. She saved all the envelopes that came addressed to her through the mails, and wrote her messages on the back of these envelopes. That relieved her of the necessity of signing her own name.

A friend of mine, Boyden Sparkes, is the co-author of a biography called *Hetty Green, A Woman Who Loved Money*. He told me that Hetty Green used to keep several million dollars on deposit at the Chemical National Bank in New York, and so she made herself at home there. She left her trunks and suitcases in the bank and she kept her old dresses and dusty rubbers in the vault. She brought an old one-horse buggy to the bank, took the wheels off, and had it stored on the second floor; and when she gave up her apartment in Hoboken, she stored her furniture in the bank.

Yet, in many ways, she had a kindly heart. For example, there was a porter at the bank, an old fellow who washed windows and ran errands and looked like a tramp. One day the bank fired him, and Hetty Green felt so sorry for him that she spent almost a week of her time getting him another job.

She died at the age of eighty-one from a stroke of paralysis, and the nurses who cared for her during her last illness were not permitted to wear their white uniforms. They wore street dresses so that Hetty would think they were ordinary servants—for the old lady could not have died peacefully had she suspected that they were expensive, trained nurses.

JOHN BARRYMORE

HE EARNED FIVE THOUSAND DOLLARS A DAY,
YET HE SEARCHED GARBAGE CANS
FOR FOOD FOR HIS PET VULTURE

ONE HOT SUMMER DAY in 1876 a young Englishman dropped in to the old Hoffman House Bar in New York and ordered a whisky and soda *without ice*. The customers at the bar were astonished to hear anyone order a drink without ice on that hot day, and they were amused at his silk hat, his monocle, and his precise Oxford accent. A gay young blade at the bar acted as a self-appointed committee of one to ridicule the English dude. Putting a silver dollar in his eye, the rich New

York socialite and athlete leaned over and said: "I say, Percy, I suppose Scotch and soda without ice is the English way, wot?"

He didn't know then that this silk-hatted chap had been the amateur lightweight boxing champion of England during his student days at Oxford. He didn't know it, but he was going to acquire the information with dramatic suddenness, for the Englishman removed his monocle carefully, pressed his silk hat more firmly on his head, and then, with extreme politeness, answered, "I beg your pardon, sir, but allow me to show you the English way." And he drove a swift haymaker to the New Yorker's jaw. When the gay blade regained consciousness, five minutes later, he shook hands with the English dude who had knocked him out and ordered drinks for everybody—drinks without ice! The crowd cheered.

This silk-hatted Englishman who packed dynamite in his punch bore a name that was destined to make American theatrical history, a name that was destined to sparkle in electric lights for years, above thousands of theaters on five continents. His name was Barrymore, Maurice Barrymore, father of the fabulous Ethel, Lionel, and John Barrymore.

The Barrymores became the most famous theatrical family of the twentieth century. They were not only famous stars on the Broadway stage, but Lionel and John became two of the most celebrated stars in Hollywood. The Barrymores were so famous that *The Royal Family,* a play about them and their relatives, was the hit of Broadway not too many years ago.

Strangely enough, none of the Barrymore children wanted to be actors. The two boys longed to be artists. Lionel disliked acting so thoroughly that he was delighted when his Grandmother Drew fired him from her production of *The Rivals,* because now he could do the thing he really wanted to do:

become an artist and paint theatrical scenery.

Lionel studied art for a while in Paris, and John got a job drawing illustrations and cartoons for Arthur Brisbane, editor of the *New York Journal*. One of his weekly assignments was to illustrate Ella Wheeler Wilcox's "Poems of Passion." John paid no attention whatever to what these poems said; he merely drew whatever amused him. For example, he once illustrated one of Mrs. Wilcox's fiery love sonnets with a drawing of a dead man hanging by a rope from the limb of a tree. Mrs. Wilcox took her literary career very seriously. She was indignant. Flying into a rage, she demanded to see the artist who was ridiculing her poetry. When the young, handsome Barrymore called at her home, the middle-aged poetess was delighted and thrilled. She invited him to tea and insisted that hereafter the charming John Barrymore must always illustrate her poems.

Three weeks later, Brisbane fired the charming John for incompetence and negligence!

One day John Barrymore and Frank Butler, a writer who lived with John and Lionel in New York (where both were trying to make a living as artists), were hungry. They had pawned a removable gold tooth belonging to Butler, but had partaken of a little entertainment and had only ten cents of their treasure left. They went to a cheap lunchroom where you could get hot cakes and two cups of coffee for ten cents. John waited outside impatiently until Butler paphad ordered the second cup of coffee and had eaten half the hot cakes. Then Barrymore dashed in and whispered in Butler's ear and Butler jumped up and moaned, "Oh! No! It can't be true! My poor mother!" He then dashed out of the lunchroom, while Jack sat down and drank the second cup of coffee and finished the hot cakes.

Lionel and Jack Barrymore were cold and hungry

in those days, but they were touched by the stuff that dreams are made on. Lionel now looks back on those days with nostalgic memories. He once composed an orchestral suite in memory of John and the days of their youth. It was played for the first time April 22, 1944, by the Philadelphia Symphony Orchestra, under the direction of Eugene Ormandy. This composition is gay in spots with the lilt of gypsy melodies and folk songs that the brothers Barrymore used to hear in a Second Avenue café when the adventure of life seemed bright and endless. Lionel declared that writing this composition seemed like having a long visit with Jack.

Maurice Barrymore collected animals of all sorts and species. Neither Lionel nor John ever lost his love of animals. A cat once had kittens in the space between the walls of Lionel's house in Hollywood, and he had a bit of the wall torn out for fear the kittens might die in that small space.

John had a pet monkey that he named Clementine. He cared for this monkey as if it were a child, took it on cruises with him, and let it eat at the same table with him.

He paid nineteen hundred dollars for two birds of paradise and spent twenty thousand dollars building an enormous aviary with a special heating apparatus to keep the air warm for his large collection of delicate tropical birds.

He once bought a huge king-vulture and made a pet of it. This vulture was as large as a goose and had a long, wicked beak. Like all vultures, it had a fondness for tainted meat. Occasionally John Barrymore, the romantic actor who drew a salary of five thousand dollars a day, would poke around Hollywood garbage cans to get the right kind of meat for his vulture. One night Barrymore, dressed in shabby working clothes, was walking along the street inspecting garbage cans. A well-dressed man saw him and mistook him for a hungry man searching in garbage cans for food for himself. The generous stranger gave Barrymore a quarter. "Be sure you spend it only for food," he advised. Barrymore touched his shabby hat humbly and murmured, "God bless you, sir!"

John Barrymore made over three million dollars in Hollywood. He made almost half a million in one year alone, the year 1931. He paid a quarter of a million for a house and almost a quarter of a million dollars for a yacht. He spent eight thousand dollars to erect a shaft with a sundial in his swimming pool. He bought a chandelier that had once hung in the palace of the Archduke Francis Ferdinand, whose assassination touched off the first World War. Barrymore paid only seventy-five dollars for the chandelier, but he spent three thousand dollars to build a room to hang it in.

In 1934 he went to India for his health. He made about 75,000 dollars that year and spent almost 300,000 dollars—four times as much as he made. The next year it was much worse. During five months of 1935, he spent at the rate of 825 dollars a day, while his income was thirty-three dollars a day. His spending was then twenty-five times as much as his income, but he was spending mostly on other people.

His intimate friend Gene Fowler says that "Barrymore cared not at all for clothes. He didn't own a watch. He wore no rings. He entertained infrequently. He much preferred to eat a herring in the kitchen, or if possible in some friend's kitchen, to sitting in costly fashion at a restaurant table. He seldom had much pocket money. Aside from his almost fierce desire to see that all his bills be paid, he did not appear to bother much about money."

Jack Barrymore had friends among the lowliest

and the highest. One of his friends was a hobo; another was Winston Churchill. It was Winston Churchill's encouragement that persuaded John Barrymore to continue his run of *Hamlet* in London after he had decided to close it.

Barrymore clowned through life with little regard for conventions. One night while playing Hamlet, he wanted to show off a bit; so between the acts he went out before the curtain dressed as Hamlet, in tights, and while a musician played a saxophone, Jack did a tap dance, a cake walk, and a waltz.

Another night, while playing a love scene in the romantic *Peter Ibbetson*, he kissed a bouquet of flowers and pressed them to his heart. A young girl in the second balcony laughed. Barrymore lost his temper and shouted, "If you think you can play this scene better than I can, come down and do it!" As he said this, he flung the bouquet into the audience and struck a woman in the face. The curtain was rung down immediately. The theater was filled with angry denunciations. The manager feared there might be a riot. The play was halted for half an hour, and before the curtain rose again the manager warned the actors to run if trouble started. When Jack walked on the stage, there was silence at first; but he won the audience immediately by his poise, charm, and brilliant acting; and a minute later the audience broke suddenly into a prolonged cheer.

On another occasion, during a flu epidemic, Barrymore was irritated by the incessant coughing of the audience. He hid a big fish under his coat and when the audience began coughing he threw the fish over the footlights and yelled, "Busy yourselves with *this*, you blasted walruses!"

Once while John was speaking the famous lines in *Richard the Third*: "A horse, a horse! My kingdom for a horse," a man in the balcony laughed loudly. Barrymore immediately pointed his sword toward the balcony and shouted, "Make haste and saddle yonder braying ass!"

John Barrymore was unquestionably one of the outstanding Hamlets of our time. He played Hamlet on Broadway longer than any other actor. So it is altogether fitting that Lionel had carved on his brother's tomb the words, "Good Night, Sweet Prince"—words uttered by Horatio as Hamlet lay dying in his arms. "Good night, sweet Prince, and flights of angels sing thee to thy rest."

ELY CULBERTSON

HE STEPPED OUTSIDE FOR A FIGHT —
WHILE HE WAS GONE HE BROKE
THE BANK AND WON $10,000!

IN THE YEAR 1921, a hot-headed young man was swaggering along the boulevards of Paris. His pockets were almost empty, but his heart was filled with boiling rage. Why? Because he had been robbed of four million dollars. Or at least his family had. Years ago, his father, an American geologist and mining engineer, had gone to Russia, discovered an oil field, and amassed a huge fortune. Then, after the war, the Soviets had confiscated his property and left him penniless. His son had fled to Paris to save his life, and there he found himself in 1921, with only twenty dollars between him and hunger.

So he took a chance. He drifted into a gambling club and bet five dollars on the game of chemin de fer. While his card was being drawn, a Frenchman stepped on his toes. He flared up like a rocket, called the French-man a swine, and demanded that he apologize *toute suite*!

Did the Frenchman apologize? He did not! He was highly insulted, and challenged the young American to a duel. They didn't have swords or pistols, so they rushed out behind the club and tore into one another with their bare fists. A couple of black eyes, a bloody nose—and then they were parted.

When the arrogant young American came back to the gambling table, he was speechless. He had broken the bank. His stake had won not only once but, while he was fighting, his winnings had kept on mounting by geometrical progression until his five dollars had been boosted into ten thousand.

That fight changed the whole course of his life—and it also affected several million Americans. How? Do you play bridge? Do you play the Culbertson system? Well, there would probably have been no Culbertson system if it hadn't been for that fist fight, for when Ely Culbertson walked into the gambling club, he intended to join the White Russian army, run his bayonet through a few Bolsheviks, and fight for the return of his property. But now with ten thousand dollars in his pocket, he forgot all about war, took the first ship to America, rushed to Washington, sued the Soviet Government for four million dollars and intended to become a novelist or a professor of economics.

That was in 1921. Culbertson was a miserable card player then. But now he takes in half a million dollars a year or ten thousand dollars a week out of the game of contract bridge. However, that's not all profit by a long shot. He spends thirty thousand dollars a year in merely answering the countless questions that are constantly fired at him by bridge fans from all over the world. His assistants answer every question without charge.

Culbertson, whose name is almost a synonym for contract bridge, was brought up by a pious Scotch Presbyterian father who taught him that all gambling was sinful and that cards were a sinister device of the devil.

A student of Karl Marx and Tolstoy, he has always been obsessed with radical ideas. Even when he was a school boy in Russia, he organized a secret Revolutionary Committee among his fellow students, and used his American passport to go to Switzerland and smuggle back forbidden copies of a Bolsheviki newspaper that Lenin was publishing in

Geneva.

When he came to America in 1922, he tried to get a job teaching philosophy and sociology; but he couldn't.

Then he tried selling coal, and he failed at that.

Then he tried selling coffee, and he failed at that.

Finally, he gave private lessons in French literature to a group of Socialists in New York and acted as concert manager for his brother, who is a violinist.

It never occurred to him to try to teach bridge then. He was only a poor card player, but a very stubborn one. He asked so many questions and held so many post mortem examinations that no one wanted to play with him. He read books about bridge, but they didn't help much, so he started to write a book himself. As the years went by, he wrote five books about bridge, but they were worthless, and he knew it, so he tore up the manuscripts before they were ever put in type. The books that he has written since then have been translated into a dozen languages and almost a million copies have been sold. One of his books has even been put into Braille so that the blind can improve their bridge games.

Culbertson first came to America in 1910. His Russian mother sent him here then because she wanted him to study at Yale. But he failed in his entrance examinations—failed because he didn't know enough English.

Think of it! He was an American citizen. He knew American history backwards and forwards. He spoke Russian, German, French, Spanish and Italian; but he couldn't get by in English. So he turned his back on Yale, drifted up to Canada, and got a job acting as a time-keeper for a gang of laborers who were building a railroad. With fiery oratory, he told them they were being cheated and underpaid, and robbed by the company stores. He stirred up trouble, organized a strike; and got himself kicked out of the company's employ.

He then walked two hundred miles to the nearest town, and beat his way to the Pacific Coast, traveling with hoboes, stealing rides on freight trains and begging for food at kitchen doors.

It is quite probable that some of the women out west who now play the Culbertson system, have handed out sandwiches and hot coffee to Ely Culbertson at their back doors.

THE WENDEL FAMILY

NEW YORK'S QUEEREST RICH FAMILY

↶ THE MOST TALKED-OF HOUSE in New York used to stand at the corner of Fifth Avenue and Thirty-ninth Street. For twenty years it was called "The House of Mystery." Detective stories, newspaper articles, plays, and even motion pictures were woven around its grim, brick walls. Fifty-thousand people passed its nailed-up front door every day for years; yet rarely did anyone ever see a sign of life behind its shuttered windows.

If you ever rode up Fifth Avenue on a sight-seeing

bus, possibly the Wendel House was pointed out to you as the only home in the world where a yard worth a million dollars was maintained so that the poodle dog would have a place to play in.

The Wendels were one of New York's richest families. Their real estate holdings were once valued at a hundred million dollars.

Yet they loved to cling to the past. A bachelor brother and his spinster sisters lived in a house that had been built when Abraham Lincoln was still an unknown prairie lawyer out in Illinois. I walked past that house when it was being razed, and saw workmen carrying out zinc bathtubs and marble wash-stands that had been in use ever since the days of slavery.

The Wendels used gas for lighting because they believed it was easier on the eyes than electricity. They had no use for radios, for dumb waiters, for elevators, or automobiles. The only modern improvement in the house was a telephone; and that was installed only two days before the death of the last of the Wendels, so that the nurse could call a doctor.

The Wendel House was assessed at only six thousand dollars; yet the lawyer often pointed out to the family that it was costing them a thousand dollars a day to live in a six-thousand-dollar house. That was true because the land on which it stood was worth almost four million dollars, and the interest on that amount plus the assessments and taxes totaled about a thousand dollars a day.

But in spite of all this wealth, the Wendel family lived in the past.

John Gottlieb Wendel died in 1914. Up to the time of his death, he had all his suits of clothes copied exactly from a suit he had purchased at the end of the Civil War.

The suit was kept in the same box in which it had

been delivered forty years earlier, and he had eighteen copies of it made at one time. He wouldn't wear any fabric that had been dyed; so, when he wanted a black suit, he got the wool from a firm in Scotland which supplied him with wool shorn especially from black sheep.

He carried an umbrella, rain or shine, winter and summer.

He had one straw hat which he wore year after year until it literally fell apart, but at the beginning of each season, he had it varnished a bright, new, shiny black.

When he invited his friends to lunch, he wrote the invitations in Latin.

He believed that all manner of mysterious diseases were contracted through the feet; so he had the soles of his shoes made of gutta-percha an inch thick to insulate him against the germs in the ground.

In his day, John Gottlieb Wendel was New York's biggest one-man landlord. He grew rich simply by sitting tight and letting the city grow up around him.

The Wendel sisters were violently opposed to drink; they once refused to sign a million-dollar lease until they were promised that the first-aid kit and the medicine cabinet to be used in the building wouldn't contain more than a pint of alcohol. In spite of that, after their death, ten thousand dollars' worth of rare wines, whiskies, and champagnes were found in their cellar. It had lain untouched for so long that hundreds of bottles had turned to vinegar.

John Gottlieb Wendel had seven sisters, and he did all in his power to keep them from marrying. He feared that if they married and had children, the estate would be broken up. So he warned them that all men were after their money, and when suitors came to call on them, he frankly told them not to call again.

Only one of the sisters, Miss Rebecca, married; and she didn't marry until she was sixty years old. The others faded into a desolate old age and died without companions. The story of their wasted lives is a pitiful illustration of how little money, in itself, can mean.

Georgianna, the most spirited of the sisters, fought against her family's restrictions until she developed a persecution mania and had to be sent away. For twenty years, she was confined to an institution for the mentally ill, and, when she died, in 1930, most of her friends thought she had been dead for years. She was worth five million dollars, but it didn't bring her five cents' worth of happiness.

Another sister, Josephine, lived alone in one of the Wendel country houses surrounded by no one but servants. The pitiful part of it is that she dreamed that the house was filled with noisy, happy children, and used to talk and play with them. She imagined that people came to see her, and she used to have her servants set six places at the dinner table. As each course was served, she would change places, pretending that she was all of the guests in turn.

One by one, as the sisters died, the rooms they had occupied were locked and the shutters closed; until finally Miss Ella left open only her bedroom, her dining-room downstairs, and the large bare room upstairs where she and her sisters had passed their lonely school days.

For years, she lived alone in that spooky, forty-room house with a few faithful old servants and her French poodle dog, Tobey.

Tobey slept in Ella's room in a little four-poster bed exactly like his mistress. And Tobey ate his dog biscuits and pork chops in the dining-room at a special brass table spread with a velvet cloth.

When Ella Wendel died, she left millions of dollars to the Methodist church for missionary work;

yet she herself had seldom gone to church.

She died believing she hadn't a living relative in the world; but within a year, presto, two thousand three hundred alleged relatives sprang up like mushrooms all over the earth.

Two hundred and ninety appeared in Tennessee alone, all clamoring for a share of her thirty-five-million-dollar estate. The German Consulate filed a blanket claim on behalf of four hundred German Wendels, and Czechoslovakia produced so many heirs that they had to be handled through the Foreign Office.

Two persons claimed to be children of John Wendel through two different secret marriages, and one of them served a sentence in jail for forging a marriage certificate and a will.

John Gottlieb Wendel never made a will. He said he "didn't want any lawyer making money out of his property." Well, the joke was on him, for before the estate was settled, not only one lawyer, but two hundred and fifty lawyers, had collected fees out of the gold-rush for the Wendel millions.

BASIL ZAHAROFF

THE MYSTERY MAN WHO MAY HAVE BEEN
RESPONSIBLE FOR THE DEATH OF SOMEONE YOU KNOW

ZAHAROFF—that was the name of one of the richest, one of the most mysterious, and one of the most bitterly condemned men on earth. A reward of a hundred thousand dollars was offered to anyone who would kill him. Numerous books were written about him; he was one of the most amazing phenomena of international suspicion and national hate.

Born in the most terrible poverty, Basil Zaharoff lived to amass one of the greatest fortunes on earth.

And he did it by selling machine guns and cannon and high explosives. One of his biographies began with these words: "The gravestones of a million men shall be his monument—their dying groans his epitaph."

When Zaharoff was twenty-eight years old, he got a job selling ammunition for $25 a week and commissions. He was living in Greece at the time; and he knew that the only way to sell guns was to create a demand for them. So he whipped up the fears of the Greeks, and told them they were surrounded by blood-thirsty enemies and must buy guns to defend their fatherland. A wave of excitement swept over the country. Bands played. Flags waved. Orators harangued the crowds; and Greece increased its army and bought guns from Zaharoff, and also a submarine—one of the first war submarines ever built.

Having made several million dollars in

commissions out of that deal, Zaharoff ran over to the Turks and said, "Look what the Greeks are doing. They are getting ready to wipe you off the face of the earth." So the Turks bought two submarines. The arms race was on, and Zaharoff had launched himself on a career that was destined to net him three hundred million dollars, all drenched with blood.

For more than half a century Zaharoff fattened on national fears, arming traditional enemies and helping to foment wars. During the Russian-Japanese conflict, he sold ammunition to both sides. During the Spanish-American War, he sold the bullets that killed American soldiers. During World War I, he owned stock in munition factories in Germany, England, France and Italy; so his wealth mounted and skyrocketed at a rate that staggers the imagination.

For half a century, he slipped in and out among

the war offices of Europe with the silence of a cat—cloaking his movements in the utmost secrecy.

He was said to have employed two men who looked precisely like him. Their sole duty was to appear in public so that the newspapers would report him in Berlin or Monte Carlo when in reality he was on a secret mission to some other city. He never willingly posed for a photograph. He never granted an interview, and he never defended, never explained, never struck back, never answered the scathing denunciations that were heaped upon him.

When he was twenty-six years old—handsome, tall, and dashing—he fell romantically in love with a young woman of seventeen. He met her on a train while traveling from Athens to Paris, and wanted to marry her at once; but she, unfortunately was already wedded to a Spanish Duke who was half-mad and twice her age. Divorce was impossible because of her religious beliefs. So Zaharoff waited for her—waited and cherished her in his heart for almost half a century. Finally, in 1923, her husband died in an insane asylum; and in 1924, she married Zaharoff. She was sixty-five at the time, and he was seventy-four years old. Two years later she died. She had been his sweetheart for forty-eight years, and his wife for eighteen months.

Until his death, he spent his summers in a magnificent chateau near Paris; but he was born in far-off Turkey in a mud hut that had no windows. As a child, he slept on a dirt floor, tied rags around his feet to keep them warm, and often went hungry.

He attended school for only five years, but he spoke fourteen languages, and Oxford University honored him with the title of Doctor of Civil Law.

The first time he appeared in London, he was jailed as a thief. Thirty years later, he was knighted by the King of England.

One day in the summer of 1909, this mystery man

of Europe was walking through the famous Zoological Gardens in Paris; and he was shocked to see that the monkeys in the Zoo were mangy and hungry, and that the most famous lion in the Zoo was suffering from rheumatism. Everything about the place seemed to be going to rack and ruin. So Zaharoff called for the manager and scolded him sharply. The manager didn't realize he was talking to one of the wealthiest men in the world, so he replied rather tartly that he didn't have the half million francs necessary to take care of the animals properly. Zaharoff said, "Well, if that's all you need, here it is," and this man whose bullets had killed a million men, wrote out a check for a hundred thousand dollars to care for some animals. The manager, unable to decipher the signature, thought the stranger was trying to play a trick on him; so he tossed the check on to a pile of other papers and forgot all about it. Months later, he showed it to a friend and was astonished to learn that it was real, that it was signed by the wealthiest man in France.

Zaharoff died at eighty-five, a lonely, tragic figure, broken in health. A servant pushed him about in a wheel chair, and his chief interest in life seemed to be his garden of lovely roses. He had been writing his diary for half a century; it filled fifty-three books; and rumor has it that he ordered all those secret records to be destroyed at his death.

LORD BYRON

THE "PERFECT LOVER" WHO CHEWED TOBACCO,
BIT HIS FINGER-NAILS,
AND DRANK WINE OUT OF HUMAN SKULLS

WHAT WAS THE PERFECT LOVER like two hundred years ago? What sort of man made our grandmothers' hearts go pit-a-pat and made our grandfathers, sitting by the fireside, twitch with a jealous apprehension? Who was the Don Juan, the Valentino, the Clark Gable of that far-off day?

The answer is easy. Two hundred years ago there was no man in the world who could compete, so far as the ladies were concerned, with the romantic George Gordon, Lord Byron.

He was the greatest poet of his day. His influence changed the whole trend of literature in the nineteenth century. He wrote some of the gustiest romantic verse to be found in our anthologies, and some of the tenderest. He loved dozens of women, but strangest of all, he loved his own half-sister, and the scandal of their love shocked Europe and ruined her life. After they were driven apart, he wrote to her one of his loveliest poems:

> *If I should meet thee*
> *After long years,*
> *How should I greet thee? —*
> *With silence and tears.*

But the more notorious Byron became, the more the women worshipped him. They worshipped him so madly that when his wife finally left him because she couldn't stand his brutality any longer, half the women of Europe denounced her. These same women deluged Byron with poems and love-letters and locks of their hair. One famous English noblewoman, an aristocrat, brilliant and wealthy, a beauty with all of London at her dainty feet, dressed herself as a boy and stood in the street for hours in the pelting rain waiting for Byron, the perfect lover, to emerge from his sacred domicile. One woman lost her head over him so completely that she followed him all the way from England to Italy and pestered him until he finally gave up.

What was he like, this great paragon of lovers, this Valentino of two centuries ago? He had a deformed foot. He limped badly. He chewed his finger-nails. He chewed tobacco. He swashbuckled about in the broad daylight of 19th century Britain bristling with loaded pistols like a Chicago gangster. His temper was vicious. If people stared at him, his blood pressure rose twenty points, for he imagined they were staring at his deformed foot. This poet who was hailed as the perfect Romeo, loved to torture women. Two hours after the marriage ceremony, he informed his bride that he hated her, that he had married her only out of spite and that she would live to rue the day she first saw him. She did.

Their connubial bonds held for one year. To be sure, he never beat her but he smashed the furniture and brought his sweethearts into the house. His wife finally called in doctors to see if he was insane.

The country people who lived near his great Abbey told strange yarns. They said that all his servants were young girls—beautiful girls, girls with amiable dispositions. The country folks told how he and his guests dressed up as monks in long black cassocks and indulged in orgies that would have made Belshazzar's dinner parties sound like a W.C.T.U, breakfast. Amiable servant girls served the wine, and Byron and his friends drank it out of *human skulls*—scraped and polished until they shone like a full moon in the desert.

Byron, slender and graceful, was often compared to the Apollo Belvedere. His skin was so white that adoring females declared that he looked "like a beautiful alabaster vase lighted up from within." But they didn't realize what agonies he went through to look like that. They didn't know that every day of his life, and every hour, was a constant, irritating, and exhausting battle against fat. In order to remain slender and lovable, he endured a diet so fantastic that it has never hit even Hollywood.

For example, he ate only one meal a day, and that one meal frequently consisted of nothing but a little potato or rice with vinegar sprinkled over it. Wanting a change, he munched a handful of dry crackers and drank a glassful of soda-water. Talk about "alabaster lighted up from within!" The miracle is that he didn't look like a Chinese skeleton in the famine district. To keep down the hated fat, he went in for fencing, boxing, horseback-riding and swimming. And this man, the greatest poet of his age, was far prouder of the fact that he had swum the Hellespont than he was of his immortal verses. When he played cricket he wore seven vests. But even seven vests didn't sweat the fat off, so three times a week he had himself pummeled and mauled in a Turkish bath.

This fantastic dieting ruined his digestion; and, as a result, his bedroom reeked of pills and potions and patent medicines. It looked more like an apothecary's shop than the seductive bower of the world's greatest lover.

He suffered so horribly from nightmares that he resorted to laudanum. But even laudanum couldn't stifle his bad dreams, so he kept two loaded pistols beside his bed. In the quiet of the night, he would wake up yelling and gnashing his teeth, and would stride up and down the room brandishing pistols and daggers.

What a story he could have written for *True Confessions* magazine. Even the *Voice of Experience* would have been stumped by the problems of his bride.

The old Abbey in which Lord Byron had his nightmares was haunted by the ghost of a long-vanished monk who had once lived there. Byron swore that this black-hooded spectre often stalked past him in the corridor with a devastating eye. He beheld this terrible apparition on the eve of his ill-fated marriage. Years later, in Italy, he swore he saw the apparition of the poet Shelley walk into a wood. Shelley himself was miles away at that moment. And Byron knew it. Curiously enough, in a short time Shelley really was dead—drowned in a storm on a lake—and Byron with his own hands built the funeral pyre and burned the body.

He had another superstition that haunted him. A gypsy fortune-teller once warned him that he would die in his thirty-seventh year. He died three months after he had passed his thirty-sixth birthday. Byron believed a sinister curse doomed all his family. The thirty-sixth birthday, he swore, was fatal to people of his blood. Some modern biographers are even inclined to agree with him for Byron's father died at the age of thirty-six, and Byron's daughter, whose life was almost exactly like her father's, also died on the eve of her thirty-sixth birthday.

Five Minute Biographies For Success
Dale Carnegie

Words & Phrases

1. Madame Curie

slap in the face 모욕
[slæp]

garret 다락방
[gǽrət]

falter 비틀거리다
[fɔ́:ltər]

sober 냉정한, 이성적인
[sóubər]

ore 광석
[ɔ:r]

leaky 물이 새는
[lí:ki]

drudgery 잡일, 허드렛일
[drʌ́dʒəri]

2. Helen Keller

blight (식물을) 마르게 하다;
[blait]
(희망 등을) 꺾다; 파괴시키다

cram 억지로 채워 넣다; 배가 터
[kræm]
지도록 먹이다

thrash 때리다, 몸부림치다
[θræʃ]

wrought 《고어》 WORK의 과거·
[rɔ:t]
과거분사

crib 구유; 아기용 침대
[krib]

elated 의기양양한, 우쭐대는
[iléitid]

prick (바늘 따위로) 찌르다
[prik]

crochet 코바늘 뜨개질, 코바늘로
[krouʃéi]
뜨개질하다

3. Andrew Carnegie

midwife 산파
[mídwàif]

bunk 잠자리, (배·기차 등의) 침
[bʌŋk]
대

dividend 나누어지는 수; 나뉜 부
[dívidènd]
분; 배당금

canny 주의 깊은, 빈틈없는
[kǽni]

belch 트림하다, (연기 등을) 뿜어
[beltʃ]
내다

4. John D. Rockefeller

hoe 곡괭이, 곡괭이질 하다
[hou]

come what might 무슨 일이 생
겨도

stamp out 근절하다, 박멸하다
[stæmp]

hookworm 십이지장충
[húkwə̀:rm]

yellow fever 황열병
[jélou fí:vər]

mantelpiece 벽난로의 앞장식
[mǽntlpì:s]

gruelling 녹초가 되게 하는
[grú:əliŋ]

uplift 들어 올리다
[ʌplíft]

round out 완성하다
[raund]

5. Mayo Brothers

insane asylum 정신병원
[inséin əsáiləm]

Holy Shrine 성묘(聖廟) cf. 여기
[hóuli ʃrain]
서는 '기적의 치료소'를 말함.

musket 머스켓 총(구식 보병총)
[mʌ́skət]

redskin (종종 경멸적으로 쓰임)
[rédskin]
미국 인디언

prairie (Mississippi 강 유역의)
[prɛ́əri]
대초원

sod 잔디, 떼
[sad]

allay 진정시키다; (고통·슬픔 등
[əléi]
을) 누그러뜨리다

smithereens 《구어》 산산조각,
[smìðəríːnz]
작은 파편

cocked hat 삼각모
[kákt hǽt]
 knock into a cocked hat
 《구어》 볼품없이 만들어 놓다, 완
 전히 때려눕히다[파괴하다]

pauper (빈민 구제법의 적용을
[pɔ́ːpər]
받는) 극빈자; 《구어》 가난뱅이

6. Enrico Caruso

mass 큰 덩어리, (천주교) 미사
[mæs]

inscrutable 불가사의한, 수수께
[inskrúːtəbl]
끼 같은

unflagging 지칠 줄 모르는
[ʌnflǽgiŋ]

shutter 셔터; 겉창문
[ʃʌ́tər]

hiss 쉿 소리를 내다
[his]

heady (술이) 취하게 하는
[hédi]

hallow 숭배하다; 신에게 바치다
[hǽlou]

warble (새가) 지저귀다; (사람이)
[wɔ́ːrbl]
목소리를 떨며 노래하다

splinter 쪼개진[부서진] 조각, 쪼
[splíntər]
개다

tipsy 《구어》 얼근히 취한; 취해서
[típsi]
비틀거리는

hoot 야유소리
[huːt]

catcall 야유소리, 날카로운 휘파람
[kǽtkɔ̀ːl]

understudy 임시 대역 배우
[ʌ́ndərstʌ̀di]

pandemonium 대혼란, 아수라장
[pæ̀ndəmóuniəm]

sear 태우다; 시들게 하다
[siər]

Evil Eye '사악한 눈' (쳐다보면
[íːvəl ái]
나쁜 일이 생긴다고 함)

spat (보통 pl.) 스패츠 (발목 조금
[spæt]
위까지 덮는 짧은 각반)

excruciating 극심한 고통을 주
[ikskrúːʃiéitiŋ]
는, 몹시 괴로운

throng 군중; 무리
[θrɔ(ː)ŋ]

pore 숙고하다, 골똘히 생각하다
[pɔːr]

7. Captain Robert Falcon Scott

crocus 크로커스 (영국에서 봄에
[króukəs]
맨 먼저 피는 꽃)

beset 에워싸다, 포위하다
[bisét]

bedevil 귀신 들리게 하다; 유혹
[bidévəl]
하다

hull 껍질, (배) 선체
[hʌl]

hold 화물칸
[hould]

gallant 씩씩한, 당당한
[gǽlənt]

trough (단면이 V자형으로 긴) 구
[trɔ(ː)f]
유, (놀과 놀 사이의) 골

flounder 버둥거리다; 허우적거
[fláundər]
리며 나아가다

treacherous 믿을 수 없는; (발
[trétʃərəs]
판·토대 등이) 불안정한, 깨지기
쉬운

crevasse 크레바스 (빙하의 갈라
[krivǽs]
진 틈)

slog 무거운 걸음걸이로 터벅터벅
[slag]
걷다

frigid 추운, 극한의
[frídʒid]

consternation 섬뜩 놀람, 소스
[kɑ̀nstərnéiʃən]
라침

tatter 넝마; 누더기옷
[tǽtər]

flaunt 자랑하다, (기 등을) 나부
[flɔːnt]
끼게 하다

frostbitten 동상에 걸린
[frɔ́ːstbitn]

heroic (pl.) 영웅시; 과장된 표현
[hiróuik]

brittle 부서지기 쉬운, 상처입기
[brítl]
쉬운

depot 저장소; 보관소
[déːpou]

ridge [ridʒ] 산마루; 능선

lash [læʃ] (밧줄·새끼줄 등으로) 묶다, 매다

8. Lawrence Tibbett

rickety [ríkiti] 낡아빠진

huzza [həzá:] (함성 소리) 와

mediocrity [mì:diákrəti] 평범

range [reindʒ] (미국) 방목 구역; 목장

rustler [rʌ́slər] 《미국 구어》 소도둑

dead shot [déd ʃát] 명사수

arsenal [á:rsənəl] 무기고; 군수 공장

bellow [bélou] 큰소리로 짖다

snub [snʌb] 윽박지르다; 무시하다

glee [gli:] 기쁨, 환희

9. William Shakespeare

shotgun [ʃʌ́tgìn] 중매 결혼의

wisdom tooth [wízdəm tù:θ] 사랑니

keep tryst with ~와 만날 약속을 지키다

paean [pí:ən] 기쁨의 노래, 찬가

idyllic [aidílik] 전원풍의; 목가적인

tempt fate [tempt feit] 운명을 시험하다, 무모한 짓을 하다

lass [læs] 여인

yeomean [jóumən] 농민

indignation [ìndignéiʃən] 분개

bond [band] 결합, 약정

farce [fa:rs] 익살극

thatched [θætʃt] 짚을 댄

hollyhock [hálihàk] 접시꽃

quaint [kweint] 기묘한, 색다른

sewer [sjú:ər] 하수구

swarm [swɔ:rm] 떼 지어 모여들다

hoarding [hɔ́:rdiŋ] 축적, 쌓기

refuse [réfju:s] 쓰레기

stable [stéibl] 마구간; 가축 우리

churn [tʃə:rn] (액체를) 교유기로 젓다

tan leather [tæn léðər] (부드럽게 하기 위해) 가죽을 무두질하다

hide [haid] (특히 큰 짐승의) 가죽

dabble (사업 등에) 잠깐 손을 대다
[dǽbəl]

bedstead 침대틀
[bédstèd]

earl 백작
[ə:rl]

the polestar 북극성
[póulstà:r]

(묘비에 새겨진 시를 현대 영어로 고치면 다음과 같음)

Good friend, for Jesus' sake forbear
to dig the dust enclosed here:
Blessed be the man that spares these stones,
and cursed be he that moves my bones.

10. Charles Dickens

fortnight 2주일간
[fɔ́:rtnàit]

audacity 대담함; 무례
[ɔ:dǽsəti]

perennial 영원한; 다년생의
[pərénjəl]

sordid 더러운, 지저분한
[sɔ́:rdid]

gutter [the~] 하층 사회, 빈민굴
[gʌ́tər]

snipe 도요새; 비열한 녀석
[snaip]

blacking 검은 구두약
[blǽkiŋ]

porridge 오트밀 죽
[pɔ́:ridʒ]

bliss (더없는) 행복, 천국의 기쁨
[blis]

fawn 아첨하다
[fɔ:n]

shoulder (책임 등을) 떠맡다
[ʃóuldər]

populace 대중
[pápjuləs]

bonfire 화톳불; 모닥불
[bɔ́nfàiər]

11. Mark Twain

newfangled 새로 나온, 신형의
[njú:fǽŋgəld]

contraption 새로운 고안; 기묘한 기계
[kəntrǽpʃən]

exchequer 국고; 재원
[ikstʃékər]

hovel 헛간; 오두막집
[hʌ́vəl]

pull through 버티어 내다

Old Man River 올드맨 리버 (미시시피 강의 별칭)

stately 위엄 있게, 당당하게
[stéitli]

kitten 새끼 고양이
[kítn]

self-accusation 자책
[sélfækjuzéiʃən]

Joan of Arc 잔다르크
[dʒóun əv á:rk]

elect 뽑힌 사람; 특권[엘리트] 계층
[ilékt]

sucker 빠는 사람[것], 《구어》 잘 속는 사람
[sʌ́kər]

headwaters 상류
[hédwɔ̀:tərz]

pulley 도르래
[púli]

set type 활자로 조판하다

set back ~을 퇴보시키다

untold 언급되어 있지 않은, 셀 수 없는
[ʌntóuld]

the Holy Land 성지
[hóuli lænd]

in a flash 순식간에, 갑자기

coachman 마부
[kóutʃmən]

lunge 찌르다; 돌진하다
[lʌndʒ]

ensue 잇따라 일어나다
[ensú:]

cuss 저주
[kʌs]

dress suit (남자의) 야회복
[drés sú:t]

air 곡조, 가락
[ɛər]

headstone 묘석
[hédstòun]

12. Martin Johnson

bloodcurdling 피를 굳게 하는, 간담을 서늘하게 하는
[blʌ́dkə̀:rdliŋ]

the Cape 희망봉 (the Cape of Good Hope)
[keip]

blatant 떠들썩한, 야단스러운
[bléitənt]

far-flung 널리 퍼진; 멀리 떨어진
[fá:rflʌ́ŋ]

stowaway 밀항자, 무임승객
[stóuəwèi]

nerve-wracking 신경을 괴롭히는, 몹시 신경질 나게 하는
[nə́:rvrækiŋ]

culinary 부엌의; 요리의
[kʌ́lənèri]

gravy 고깃국물
[gréivi]

billow 큰 물결, 큰 물결이 치다
[bílou]

nautical 항해의
[nɔ́:tikəl]

whoop 아아[우아] 하는 외침. 고함지르다
[hu(:)p]

cockeyed 사팔뜨기의, 《속어》 어리석은
[kákàid]

sizzling 지글지글 소리 내는; 《구어》 몹시 더운
[sízəliŋ]

molasses 당밀, 사탕수수 시럽
[məlǽsiz]

cannibal 식인종
[kǽnəbəl]

veldt 아프리카 남부의 초원지대
[velt]

spool [spu:l] 실감개; (필름·녹음테이프 등의) 릴; 한 번 감은 양

unreel [ʌnríːl] 실패에서 풀다; 릴에 감긴 필름을 풀다

twitch [twitʃ] (소매 등을) 홱 잡아당기다, 씰룩거리다

whisker [hwískər] 구레나룻, (고양이·쥐 등의) 부리 둘레의 털

cavalcade [kæ̀vəlkéid] 기마대; 기마 행진

home stretch 마지막 직진 주로

close call 《구어》 위기일발, 구사일생

kettle [kétl] 솥

chop [tʃap] 자르다, 《서아프리카·구어》 음식

13. Florenz Ziegfeld

firmament [fə́ːrməmənt] 《문어》 창공, 하늘

revue [rivjúː] 레뷰(익살스러운 뮤지컬 코미디의 일종)

regal [ríːgəl] 제왕의; 제왕 같은

extravagance [ikstrǽvəgəns] 사치스러움

potentate [póutəntèit] 군주; 유력자

profligate [práfligət] 방탕한, 낭비하는

pulchritude [pʌ́lkrətjùːd] 《문어》 (특히 여자의) 몸매의 아름다움

vivacious [vivéiʃəs] 활기[생기] 있는, 쾌활한

scintillating [síntəlèitiŋ] 생기발랄한

palpitating [pǽlpətèitiŋ] 가슴이 뛰는, 가슴 벅찬

skyrocket [skáirɑ̀kit] 갑자기 높이 날아오르다; (명성 등이) 높아지다

sweet pea [swiːt piː] 스위트피(콩과의 원예 식물)

orchid [ɔ́ːrkid] 난초

licorice [líkərəs] 감초

jam [dʒæm] 채워 넣다, (장소·통로를) 막다[메우다]

ermine [ə́ːrmin] 흰담비

wardrobe [wɔ́ːrdròub] 옷장, 의상

auspicious [ɔːspíʃəs] 길조의, 상서로운

tinsel [tínsəl] 반짝거리는 금속 조각

pageant 야외극, 구경거리
[pǽdʒənt]

delirium 섬망 상태, (일시적) 정신 착란
[dilíriəm]

valet 시종
[vǽlit]

parch 바짝 마르게 하다
[pɑːrtʃ]

14. Howard Thurston

headliner 신문의 표제를 쓰는 기자, 《미·속어》 주요 연기자
[hédlàinər]

unvarnished 니스를 칠하지 않은; 소박한
[ʌnvάːrniʃt]

hobo 뜨내기 일꾼; 부랑자
[hóubou]

box car 《미》 화물 열차
[bάks kὰːr]

jockey 경마 기수
[dʒάki]

evangelist 복음 전도자, 복음 설교자
[ivǽndʒəlist]

erstwhile 《고어》 이전에, 옛날에
[ə́ːrsthwàil]

tramp 쾅쾅거리며 걷다, 부랑자
[træmp]

popeyed 《놀라움 등으로》 눈이 휘둥그레한
[pάpàid]

flood tide 밀물, 최고조
[flʌ́d tὰid]

bill as (전단·벽보 등에) ~로 소개[광고]되다
[bil]

15. William Randolph Hearst

solitaire 《미》 혼자 하는 카드놀이
[sάlitɛ̀ər]

reticent 과묵한; 말이 적은
[rétəsənt]

hobnob 친하게[격의 없이] 사귀다
[hάbnὰb]

ranch 대목장, 농장
[ræntʃ]

rockbound 바위로 둘러싸인
[rάkbὰund]

Moorish 무어 양식의
[múəriʃ]

tapestry 태피스트리(벽걸이 융단)
[tǽpistri]

chateau (pl. chateaus, chateaux) 성; 큰 저택
[ʃætóu]

snarl (개 등이) 으르렁거리다
[snɑːrl]

Forty-nine 여기서는 1849년을 뜻함
[fɔ́ːrtinàin]

clog dance 나막신 춤
[klάg dæ̀ns]

phraseology 어구; 표현
[frèiziάlədʒi]

16. Lionel Barrymore

has-been 한창때가 지난 사람, 과

거의 사람[물건]

The Copperhead copperhead
[kápərhèd]
는 '살모사'란 뜻. 이 글에서는 브
로드웨이의 연극 제목

rumbling 울리는, 광광거리는
[rʌ́mbliŋ]

haphazard 우연한; 계획성 없
[hæphæ̀zərd]
는, 아무렇게나

escapade 탈선 행위; 엉뚱한 행위
[éskəpèid]

dilapidated 낡아빠진, 황폐한
[diláepədèitid]

boardinghouse 기숙사; 하숙집;
[bɔ́:rdiŋ hàus]
숙소

Camille 베르디의 오페라 〈춘희〉
[kǽnəmail]

chap 갈라진 금, 금이 생기게 하
[tʃæp]
다, 《주로 영·구어》 놈, 녀석

17. Somerset Maugham

morbid 병적인, 무서운
[mɔ́:rbid]

rip-roaring 《구어》 떠들썩한, 법
[ríprɔ̀riŋ]
석을 떠는

swerve 벗어나게 하다, 벗어나다
[swə:rv]

smash hit 대성공(히트)
[smǽʃ hit]

[kəpǽsəti haus]

capacity house 《미》(사람들로)
만원인 건물(cf. 여기서는 관객으
로 가득 찬 극장)

toast 건배, 건배를 받는 사람, 인
[toust]
기인

mantel 벽난로의 앞장식, 벽난로
[mǽntl]
선반

18. Clarence Darrow

fidgety 《구어》 안절부절 못하는,
[fídʒiti]
조바심하는

squirm (벌레 같이) 꿈틀거리다;
[skwə:rm]
몸부림치다

criminal lawyer 형사소송 전문
[krímənl lɔ́:jər]
변호사

underdog 싸움에 진 개; 패배자
[ʌ́ndərdɔ̀(:)g]

old-timer 《구어》 고참자; 구식
[óuldtáimər]
사람 《미》 노인

cuss 저주; 놈, 녀석
[kʌs]

tinsmith 함석장이, 양철공
[tínsmiθ]

spellbinder 《미》 웅변가; (특히)
[spélbàindər]

청중을 매료하는 연설가[정치가]

scrap [skræp] 조각, 다툼, 다투는 사람

thumb through 급히 훑어보다

Blackstone [blǽkstoun] 영국의 판사 겸 법률서적 저술가; (블랙스톤의) 법률서적

yearly installment [jɚrli instɔ́:lmənt] 연간 할부

point-blank [pɔ́intblǽŋk] 직사(直射)의, 딱 잘라

revile [riváil] 욕하다, 헐뜯다

19. Clyde Beatty

maul [mɔ:l] (큰 망치로 상처가 나도록) 치다, 〈짐승 등이〉 할퀴어 상처내다

gore [gɔːr] (소·산돼지 등이) 뿔로 찌르다[들이받다]

big top [bíg tɑ́p] 《구어》 (서커스의) 큰 천막

chug [tʃʌg] (소리를 내며) 천천히 떠나가다

not worth a plugged nickel 《미·속어》 아무 가치도 없는

bristle [brísl] (털 등을) 곤두세우다, (화·용기 등을) 불러일으키다

hoot [hu:t] 울음소리를 내다, 《구어》 무가치한 것, 조금

Mae West [méi wést] 마에 웨스트 (미국의 여배우이자 섹스 심벌)

reckless [réklis] 앞뒤를 가리지 않는, 무모한

halitosis [hæ̀lətóusis] 《병리》 구취(口臭), 입냄새

cartridge [káːrtridʒ] (총) 약실, 카트리지

get someone's goat 《구어》 ~를 화나게 하다, 약올리다

pamper [pǽmpər] 욕망을 한껏 채워 주다; 응석을 받아 주다

pet [pet] (동물을) 애완용으로 삼다; (사람·동물에 대해) 응석을 받아 주다

gang up 《구어》 단결하여 대항하다

pedestal [pédəstl] 받침대

somersault 공중돌기, 공중제비
[sʌ́mərsɔ̀:lt]

haul off 물러나다, 후퇴하다

20. Ely Culbertson

break the bank (노름판에서) 물주의 돈을 휩쓸다

hotheaded 성급한, 성마른
[hɑ́thédid]

swaggering 뽐내며 걷는; 뻐기는
[swǽgəriŋ]

boulevard 넓은 가로수길; 《미》
[bú(:)ləvɑ̀:rd]
큰길, 대로

chemin de fer 슈맹드페르 (카드 게임의 일종)

toute suite (불어) 즉시, 당장

bridge 브리지 《카드놀이의 일종》
[bridʒ]

bayonet 총검
[béiənit]

not by a long shot 조금도 ~ 않다

smuggle 밀수입[밀수출]하다, 몰
[smʌ́gl]
래 갖고 들어오다

postmortem 사후(死後)의; 사후
[poustmɔ́:rtəm]
(事後)의

Braille 점자(법)
[breil]

oratory 웅변(술); 연설
[ɔ́:rətɔ̀:ri]

21. Leo Tolstoy

venerate 존경하다
[vénərèit]

garment 의복
[gɑ́:rmənt]

mince 잘게 썰다, 점잔빼며 조금
[mins]
씩 걷다

trundle (바퀴·수레 등이) 돌다,
[trʌ́ndl]
구르다

wheelbarrow 일륜차(一輪車)
[hwí:lbæ̀rou]

plaudit [보통 pl.] 갈채; 칭찬
[plɔ́:dət]

frivolous 천박한, 경박한
[frívələs]

nag 괴롭히다
[næg]

veritable 실제의, 정말의
[vérətəbl]

wither 《시어·문어》 어디로, 어
[wíðər]
느 곳으로

22. J. Pierpont Morgan

easter lily 《미》 부활절 장식용
[í:stər líli]
백합

Mogul [móugʌl] 《특히 인도에 제국을 세운》 무굴 사람, 중요 인물, 거물

shun [ʃʌn] (사람을) 피하다, (세상을) 멀리하다

indiscretion [ìndiskréʃən] 무분별, 지각없음; 경솔한 언동

dodge [dadʒ] (재빨리) 피하다, 날쌔게 비키다

wrench [rentʃ] 비틀기, 비틀다

squat [skwat] 웅크리다, 쪼그리고 앉다, 쪼그리고 앉은 자세

citadel [sítədl] 성(城); 요새

hideous [hídiəs] 끔찍한, 섬뜩한

decrepit [dikrépit] 노쇠한, (건물 등이) 오래 써서 낡은

saffron [sǽfrən] 【식물】 사프란, 샛노랑

shrapnel [ʃrǽpnəl] 유산탄

hurl [həːrl] 세게 내던지다

ledge [ledʒ] (벽·창 등에서 내민) 선반

maim [meim] (손·발을 잘라) 불구로 만들다

shriek [ʃriːk] 비명을 지르다

headlong [hédlɔːŋ] 곤두박이로, 거꾸로

bedlam [bédləm] 대소동; 소란한 곳

dastardly [dǽstərdli] 비열한

ransom [rǽnsəm] (포로의) 몸값, 배상금

sanctum [sǽŋktəm] (유대 신전의) 성소(聖所)

unostentatious [ʌ̀nɑstentéiʃəs] 거만 떨지 않는, 순박한, 수수한

soot [sut] 그을음, 매연(煤煙)

Episcopal [ipískəpəl] 성공회의

illuminated manuscript [ilúːmənèitid mǽnjəskrìpt] 채식(彩飾) 사본

folio [fóuliòu] 전지(全紙)의 2절, 2절판 《책 가운데 제일 큰 것》

connoisseur [kɑ̀nəsə́ːr] (미술품 등의) 감정가, 감식가

succumb [səkʌ́m] (유혹 등에) 굴복하다 (병·부상 등으로) 죽다 (~ to)

23. Evangeline Booth

spinster [spínstər] 미혼 여성

snort [snɔːrt] (말이) 콧김을 뿜다

buck [bʌk] 수사슴, (말이 갑자기 등을 굽히고) 뛰어오르다

the Bowery [báuəri] 바워리 (뉴욕 시의 큰 거리로 싸구려 술집과 여관이 모여 있음)

the Salvation Army [sælvéiʃən áːrmi] (자선단체) 구세군

sheaf [ʃiːf] 묶음, 다발

seethe [siːð] 끓어오르다, (화·흥분 등으로) 들끓다

horde [hɔːrd] 유목민의 무리; 군중

Dillinger 딜린저 (존 딜린저. 악명 높은 범죄자로서 FBI에 의해 사살됨)

posse [pɑ́si] 무장보안대

tartlet [táːrtlit] 작은 파이

Pullman [púlmən] 풀만식 침대차

porter [pɔ́ːrtər] 《미》 침대차(식당차)의 급사

24. Billy Sunday

sawdust [sɔ́ːdʌst] 톱밥(sawdust trail : 종교적 회개 의식을 위해 설치한 길)

pulpit [púlpit] 설교단, 설교자

boozefighter [búːzfàitər] 금주운동가

lambaste [læmbéist] 《구어》 몹시 때리다

Prohibition [pròuhəbíʃən] (미국) 금주령

dynamo [dáinəmòu] 발전기

thump [θʌmp] (특히 주먹으로) 쾅쾅 치다

pummel [pʌ́məl] 주먹으로 치다

rub-down [rʌbdaun] 신체 마찰, 마사지

en masse 한꺼번에

rube [ruːb] 《속어》 시골뜨기

proboscis [proubɑ́sis] (곤충 따위의 긴) 주둥이; 《구어·우스개》 (사람의) 큰 코

gunny sack [gʌ́nisæ̀k] 굵은 삼베 자루

saucer [sɔ́ːsər] 찻잔 받침 접시

hypnotic [hipnɑ́tik] 최면을 거는, 최면 상태인

tank up 《속어》 진탕 마시다(먹다)

tabernacle [tǽbərnæ̀kl] 유대 신전, 회당

25. Theodore Roosevelt

wielded a big stick 강권을 휘두르다

pitch 내던지다, (건초를) 쌓아올리다
[pitʃ]

farmhand 농장노동자, 머슴
[fáːrmhænd]

libel (문서에 의한) 명예훼손
[láibəl]

the Executive Mansion 대통령 관저
[igzékjutiv mǽnʃən]

hollow 속이 빈, 움푹한
[hάlou]

26. Woodrow Wilson

consecrate 신성하게 하다, 전념하다
[kάnsikrèit]

unbend 곧게 펴다, 긴장을 풀다
[ʌnbénd]

bleacher 표백업자; 《야구 속어》 야구장의 외야석
[blíːtʃər]

chromo 다색 석판인쇄
[króumou]

highbrow 지식인, 지식인인 체하는
[háibràu]

cloister 수도원에 가두다
[klɔ́istər]

edify 교화시키다; 품성을 기르다
[édəfài]

lapel (양복의) 접은 옷깃
[ləpél]

reface 수리하다, 수선하다
[riféis]

satin (비단·나일론 등의) 공단
[sǽtən]

sable 검은담비
[séibl]

27. Jack London

vagrancy 부랑죄
[véigrənsi]

penitentiary (가톨릭) 고해소, (미국) 교도소
[pènəténʃəri]

bum 부랑자, 룸펜
[bʌm]

panhandler 《미국 구어》 거지
[pǽnhændl]

cream 크림, 정화(精華), 정수, the cream of society 최상층 사회, 사교계의 꽃
[kriːm]

longshoreman (미국) 항만[부두] 노동자
[lɔ́ːŋʃɔ́ːrmən]

tramp 부랑자, 뜨내기 일꾼
[træmp]

hoodlum 《구어》 건달, 깡패
[húːdləm]

waterfront 해안[강가] 구역; 부두, 선창
[wɔ́ːtərfrʌ̀nt]

Words & Phrases

play hookey 학교를 빼먹다, 꾀를 부려 쉬다

28. Chic Sale

The Good Earth (펄벅의 소설) 대지

vulgar 천박한
[vʌ́lgər]

grease paint (배우가 쓰는) 화장용 기름
[griːs pèint]

railroad shop 철도 제작소
[réilròud ʃap]

footlights 각광, 무대
[fútlàits]

telescope suitcase 접이식 여행 가방
[téləskòup súːtkèis]

stutter 말을 더듬다
[stʌ́tər]

husker 탈곡기
[hʌ́skər]

29. Yeats-Brown

lancer 창기병
[lǽnsər]

Vedanta (인도) 베단타 철학
[vidάːntə]

engrossing 마음을 빼앗는, 몰두시키는
[ingróusiŋ]

dashing 용감한; 화려한
[dǽʃiŋ]

lordly 당당한; 위엄 있는
[lɔ́ːrdli]

crack 갈라진 틈, 《영·구어》 일류의 사람[물건]; 제일인자
[kræk]

regiment (군사) 연대, 부대
[rédʒəmənt]

embue (imbue) (사상·정신을) 고취시키다
[imbjúː]

polo 폴로(말을 타고 하는 공치기)
[póulou]

bramble 검은 딸기; 가시 관목
[brǽmbəl]

boar 수퇘지, 멧돼지
[bɔːr]

trotter 빨리 달리는 말
[trάtər]

whinny 힝힝 울어대다
[hwíni]

heave 올리다, 높아지다
[hiːv]

tear for ~를 향해 쏜살같이 달리다

mash 짓이기다, 엉망진창으로 부수다
[mæʃ]

vermin-infested 해충이 득실거리는
[və́ːrmininféstid]

governess 여자 가정교사
[gʌ́vərnis]

flirtation 연애
[fləːrtéiʃən]

doll up 화려하게 차려입다

picture hat 테 넓은 여성 모자
[píktʃər hæt]

veil 면사포
[veil]

muff 머프 (원통형의 모피로 양손
[mʌf]
을 그 속에 넣는 여성용 토시)

knowingly 안다는 듯이
[nóuiŋli]

Mademoiselle Josephine 마
[mædəmwəzél dʒóuzəfi:n]
드모아젤 조세핀 (여자 인형의 일
종. 여기서는 변장한 여자정교사
차림)

derby hat 중산 모자
[dá:rbi hæt]

the real McCoy 《구어》 (가짜가
[rí:əl məkɔ́i]
아닌) 틀림없는 본인, 진짜

slink 살금살금 걷다
[sliŋk]

buzzard 대머리수리
[bʌ́zərd]

30. Al Jolson

stenographer's stipend 속기
[stənágrəfərs stáipend]
사의 급여, 낮은 보수

sanitarium 요양소
[sænətɛ́əriəm]

not ~ half 조금도 ~않다

flush 물이 쏟아지다, 활기를 띠게
[flʌʃ]
하다

Ghetto 유대인 강제 거주 구역;
[gétou]
빈민가

kosher 유대인의 법률에 맞는, 정
[kóuʃər]
결한

synagogue 유대교 회당
[sínəgɔ:g]

thicket 수풀, 덤불
[θíkit]

raw 날 것의, 따끔따끔하게 아픈
[rɔ:]

nickel 니켈, 돈
[níkəl]

delirious 정신 착란의; 기뻐서
[dilíriəs]
흥분하는

31. Sinclair Lewis

mackerel 고등어
[mǽkərəl]

weakfish 민어
[wí:kfiʃ]

hit the bull's-eye 정곡을 찌르
다, 대성공을 거두다

repercussion 반격
[rì:pərkʌ́ʃən]

smart aleck 교만한 사람; 우쭐
[smá:rt ǽlik]
대는 사람

Words & Phrases 331

dash off 쏟아내다

lumberjack 나무꾼
[lʌ́mbərdʒæ̀k]

swanky 멋진, 화려한
[swǽŋki]

chuck 휙 던지다
[tʃʌk]

steerage (배의) 3등 선실
[stíərid3]

Red Grange 레드 그렌지 (전설적인 미국의 미식축구 선수)

phony 가짜
[fóuni]

flabbergast 깜짝 놀라게 하다
[flǽbərgæ̀st]

32. Diamond Jim Brady

Haroun Al Raschid 하룬 알 라쉬드(페르시아 아비시드 왕조 시대의 가장 유명한 군주)

dine 만찬을 베풀다
[dain]

whoop it up 《속어》와 하고 떠들어대다; 무턱대고 칭찬하다

riotous 폭동의; 먹고 마시며 떠드는
[ráiətəs]

knickknack 작은 물건; 자질구레한 장신구
[níknæk]

memento 기념품
[miméntou]

Good-time Charlie 굿타임 찰리(술과 여성 행각으로 유명했던 미국 정치인 찰스 네스빗 윌슨의 별명)
[gúdtaim tʃá:rli]

Mother Goose 머더 구스 (영국의 전승 동요집의 작가 또는 그 작품)
[mʌ́ðər gúːs]

squander (시간·돈 등을) 낭비하다
[skwɑ́ndər]

inconsequential 중요하지 않은
[inkɑ̀nsikwénʃəl]

stein 맥주잔
[stain]

root beer 루트 비어(알코올 성분이 거의 없는 맥주의 일종)
[rúːt bìər]

bottommost 밑에 있는
[bɑ́təmmòust]

lariat 던지는 올가미
[lǽriət]

bedeck 덮다; 장식하다
[bidék]

bespangle 흩뿌리다, 번쩍이게 하다
[bispǽŋgəl]

scintillating 번쩍이는
[síntəlèitiŋ]

shirt stud 셔츠의 장식단추

preposterous 앞뒤가 맞지 않
[pripástərəs]
는; 터무니없는

gala 축제
[géilə]

pail 통
[peil]

carnelian (보석) 홍옥수
[ka:rní:ljən]

lapis lazuli (보석) 청금석
[lǽpis lǽzjulài]

onyx (보석) 마노
[ániks]

mother-of-pearl (보석) 진주모

handcar (미국) (선로 보수용의)
[hǽndkà:r]
작은 수동기차

stovepipe 난로 연통
[stóuvpàip]

I.O.U 차용증서
[àiòujú:]

33. Hetty Green

scrubwoman 잡역부
[skrʌ́bwùmən]

outright 현금을 내고서
[áutràit]

lock, stock, and barrel

이것저것

berth 침대, 침대칸
[bə:rθ]

daycoach 《미》 보통 객차
[déikòutʃ]

evening wrap 외출용 목도리, 숄
[í:vniŋ ræp]

wedge 쐐기, V자 모양의 것
[wedʒ]

tenderloin 안심
[téndərlòin]

junk man 《미》 고철상, 고물상
[dʒʌ́ŋk mæn]

dodge 회피하다
[dadʒ]

half the time 《구어》 자주, 대개

vault 지하 금고
[vɔ:lt]

buggy 마차
[bʌ́gi]

34. Maurice Barrymore

monocle 외눈안경
[mánəkəl]

dude 멋쟁이, 맵씨꾼
[dju:d]

socialite 사교계의 명사
[sóuʃəlàit]

wot '알다, 알고 있다'란 뜻의 고어
[wat]
wit의 1인칭·3인칭 단수 현재형

haymaker 건초 만드는 사람,
[héimèikər]
《속어》 녹아웃 펀치, 강타

partake (식사 따위를) 함께 하다
[pa:rtéik]

Jack (John의 애칭)
[dʒæk]

lilt 경쾌한 가락
[lilt]

aviary 조류 사육장
[éivièri]

shabby 초라한, 추레한
[ʃǽbi]

Words & Phrases **333**

sundial 해시계
[sʌ́ndàiəl]

archduke (귀족) 대공
[a:rtʃdúːk]

herring 청어
[hériŋ]

cake walk 스탭댄스
[kéik wɔ́ːk]

poised 침착한; 균형 잡힌
[pɔizd]

yonder 저쪽의(에)
[jándər]

bray (당나귀가) 시끄럽게 울다
[brei]

flights 무리, 떼
[flaits]

35. Wendel FAMILY

nailed-up (문·창 등을) 못질하다

raze 지우다; (건물을) 무너뜨리다
[reiz]

zinc 아연
[ziŋk]

shorn 베어낸, 잘라낸(cf. shear
[ʃɔːrn]
　의 과거분사)

varnish 니스 칠을 하다
[váːrniʃ]

sole 발바닥; 구두의 창
[soul]

gutta-percha 구타페르카(나무
[gʌ́tə pə́ːrtʃə]
　진으로 만든 고무와 비슷한 물질)

sit tight 《구어》침착한 자세를 갖

다, 사태를 가만히 바라보다

suitor 제소인, 구혼자
[súːtər]

persecution mania 피해망상
[pə̀ːrsikjúːʃən mèiniə]

spooky 《구어》유령 같은; 무시무
[spúːki]
　시한

Methodist 감리교 신자, 감리교의
[méθədist]

36. Basil Zaharoff

epitaph 묘비명
[épətæ̀f]

orator 연설자, 강연자
[ɔ́(ː)rətər]

harangue 열변을 토하다
[hərǽŋ]

cloak 외투, 외투를 입히다, (사
[klouk]
　상·목적 등을) 가리다, 숨기다

scathing 냉혹한, 통렬한
[skéiðiŋ]

denunciation 비난
[dinʌ̀nsiéiʃən]

mangy 누추한, 더러운
[méindʒi]

tartly 신랄하게
[táːrtli]

37. Lord Byron

twitch 뒤틀다
[twitʃ]

gusty 돌풍의; 세찬; 용기 있는
[gʌ́sti]

half sister 이복 여동생
[hǽf sìstər]

deluge 범람하게 하다, 쏟아 붓다
[délju:dʒ]

lock 머리 타래
[lak]

dainty 고상한, 우아한
[déinti]

pelting 《고어》 시시한, 하찮은
[péltiŋ]

domicile 거소, 숙소
[dáməsàil]

pester 괴롭히다
[péstər]

paragon 모범, 전형
[pǽrəgàn]

swashbuckle 허세부리며 걷다
[swáʃbÀkl]

out of spite 악의로

rue 후회하다
[ru:]

connubial 결혼의; 부부의
[kənjú:biəl]

cassock 성직자의 복장
[kǽsək]

orgy 유흥, 방탕
[ɔ́:rdʒi]

alabaster 앨러배스터석
[ǽləbæ̀stər]

hit even Hollywood 할리우드 배우에도 적합하지 않다

munch 우적우적 먹다
[mʌntʃ]

reek of ~냄새가 나다

potion 마시는 약
[póuʃn]

patent medicine 처방전 없이 살 수 있는 약
[pǽtənt médəsin]

apothecary 약국
[əpάθəkèri]

bower 거처
[báuər]

laudanum 아편 팅크, 아편제
[lɔ́:dənəm]

gnash 이를 갈다
[gnæʃ]

brandish 휘두르다
[brǽndiʃ]

stump 그루터기, 그루터기를 뽑다, 근절하다
[stʌmp]

apparition 망상, 환영
[æ̀pəríʃn]

pyre 화장용(火葬用) 장작
[páiər]

Words & Phrases **335**